How to Make Japanese Management Methods Work in the West

KAZUO MURATA
(Yuasa Battery Co Ltd)

with
Alan Harrison
(Warwick Business School)

Gower

First published in hardback 1991 by Gower Publishing. Reprinted 1993.

This paperback edition published 1995 by
Gower Publishing
Gower House
Croft Road
Aldershot
Hants GU11 3HR
England

Gower
Old Post Road
Brookfield
Vermont 05036
USA

British Library Cataloguing in Publication Data
Murata, Kazuo
    How to make Japanese management methods work in the West.
    1. Great Britain. Industries. Management. Influence of management of Japanese industries
    I. Title   II. Harrison, Alan
    658.00941

Library of Congress Cataloguing-in-Publication Data
Murata, Kazuo
    How to make Japanese management methods work in the
    West / Kazuo Murata; with Alan Harrison
        p.   cm
    1. Industrial management – Japan. 2. Corporations, Japanese
    – Great Britain – Case studies. I. Harrison, Alan   II. Title
    HD70.J3M84   1991
    658 – dc20   90-19372
                                                           CIP

ISBN 0 566 09085 6 (Hbk)
      0 566 07675 6 (Pbk)

Printed in Great Britain at the University Press, Cambridge

HOW TO MANAGE
MANAGEMENT
WORK IN THE WEST

Contents

Figures and Tables

Tables

Foreword

In March 1989 I escorted a group of Tunisian workers, members of a Quality Control circle, to Yuasa Battery, UK at Ebbw Vale for a study of its quality circle activities. While those activities were impressive, what was even more impressive to our group was the Managing Director of the company himself. The Managing Director, Mr Kazuo Murata, had already become well known in Tunisia.

I had received a letter from Mr B. S. Belkhiria of the Tunis-Asia Institute. He wanted me to go over there to transplant the quality circle concept from Japan in the hope that it would destroy the class distinction in their society which had developed during the French colonization. Although I was not sure whether I could achieve anything useful, in any case I started my efforts in Tunisia.

At about the same time, I became acquainted with Mr Murata when both of us were invited to the Japan week held in Wales. Although he could not claim to be the most eloquent of speakers, his tone, the warmth of his eyes and his words too radiated something very important for management. Therefore at his invitation I made an instant decision to go and see how he was doing.

On that morning I could not indulge in the British luxury of a cup of tea. When the clock struck ten, Mr Murata ran into the factory with heavy boots on and started to wash and clean the floor! After that, he started 'management by walking about' to greet and talk with every employee. On one operator's desk he found some metal dust. Then he took up a vacuum hose to clean it himself. The operator tried to do it too. But the Managing Director said to him "Please continue your work – this is something I can do!" From this I developed a lesson for the top management in Tunisia:

> 'When you walk about in your factory and you find something which you can do and which your workers cannot do without stopping the production line, which is better for your company – you do it yourself, or you make them do it?'

This was a lesson not only in efficiency, but also in breaking down barriers between staff and shop floor.

What Mr Murata did always had a rationale behind it. For example, his desk was just one of many managers' desks in a big open room. This might be taken to be a symbol of the Japanese egalitarian spirit. But it was not only a spiritual matter. It also facilitated communication. Oral communication is much quicker and more open than paper communication between compartments.

However, oral communication is not always effective in helping people to understand. In order to compensate for this drawback, Mr

Murata invented a 'display room' where all aspects of company performance information were displayed on panels in the form of graphs and tables. The display room is open to any member of the company. And a company member who is responsible for certain pieces of information has to explain them to other company members if requested. Mr Murata made his management systems openly visible.

I believe that the management systems thus created by Mr Murata are not purely Japanese. Until he was sent to the UK he had been a scientist in R & D all his life. To be frank, it was fortunate that he had not experienced the full force of Japanese management. As a scientist, Mr Murata extracted good elements of management from around the world including Japan, and blended them in his own brew of logic and humanism.

In Tunisia I have used the story of Mr Murata as a textbook for the management of her industries. That is why Mr Murata is already well known there. Those workers who were impressed by their visit to the UK are now making every effort to improve their factory to an equivalent level. Their Managing Director is also trying to become a Murata in Tunisia.

The Murata system has been accepted by the British, the Tunisians and the Japanese. So I am confident that its cross-cultural appeal will make it popular in countries around the world, and that it will therefore contribute to the betterment of industrial society.

Professor Naoto Sasaki
Graduate School of Systems Management
Tsukuba University, Tokyo

Preface

Another Five Nations Rugby Championship has come and gone and those who have not experienced Cardiff city centre on an international day have missed an education in enthusiasm and commitment.

It is difficult to describe the atmosphere and passion of the occasion unless you are actually there at Cardiff Arms Park. A throng of young people moves towards the ground, singing and chanting with much good humour. I have never experienced in my lifetime such emotional excitement as the atmosphere in an international match environment. Inside the ground young and old join in the traditional singing which culminates in the Welsh national anthem. The voices swell as one with the united passion of one nation. Being there and listening to the supporters and feeling the emotion that grips all in the stadium one understands that mental attitude and commitment are wonderful attributes (Figure P.1).

This is the atmosphere that industry wants to create. People in the crowd watch the players' every action as if they were playing themselves. There is a great surge of energy and enjoyment of life in these players as they create alert, winning movements under strict rules and under tremendous physical and emotional pressure. I wanted to develop the same atmosphere in my company. This would form the ideal business atmosphere, where people regard the company in the same way as they regard the international at Cardiff Arms Park. In business it is just as important to achieve a team spirit with a united desire to win. Furthermore the quality of life during work is of paramount importance, and the extension and utilization of individual skills and creativity should be promoted in just the same way as they are in a rugby international.

If the sole purpose of a business is to make money, it will be very difficult to make that company an excellent one. Only when each company member achieves the status of international player will the company become excellent, with long-term prosperity the reward.

I have always borne such an ideal company status in mind, and have tried to achieve it. After seven-and-a-half years my company is still progressing towards the ideal, but I have taken many initiatives to work towards company excellence, and now I would like to share my ideas with others in British industry and with the community which I loved, as an expression of thanks to this beautiful country of Wales. I would also like to leave a record of these ideas with our British colleagues, who can refer to them as they continue their efforts to make Yuasa Battery (UK) Limited an excellent company.

I would like to acknowledge the encouragement we were given by the receipt of the Queen's Award for Export Achievement by our company after only three years in production, and the conditions under which

Figure P.1   Welsh rugby supporters at the Arms Park — a lesson in unity and passion

our company can flourish. I am leaving this beautiful part of the world after seven and a half years, which means that – in terms of my adult life – I am 20 per cent Welsh!

Companies all over the world run their own business in their own way, and this is just one example of a successful experience. But it is my strong hope that our experience will contribute to the development of British industry, and to the entrepreneur who wants to establish business in this country. Many manufacturers throughout the world are at present adopting what they believe to be 'Japanese' working methods, without realizing that good working practices are basically a matter of common sense and a correct approach to the working environment. This book outlines the various ideas which we created and successfully installed that have established this company as the leader in its field in Europe.

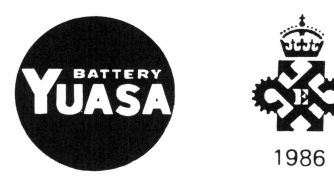

Figure P.2   Company and Queen's Award for Export Achievement logos

Acknowledgements

I am very pleased to have the opportunity to publish this book. If it makes a small contribution to British industry, in which I have worked hard and which I have enjoyed so much, I will be amply rewarded. Company members from Yuasa Battery (UK) Limited, Mr Ian Taylor (Chief Accountant) and Mr Mike Holmes (General Manager) have rewritten my draft into good English and Mrs Mary Matthews (Technical Section) kindly made the lively illustrations. All three have striven for years to make our company an excellent one, and have now joined with me to record our achievements in this book, demonstrating soundness and flexibility in work outside their normal jobs.

I am sure that this book would not have come out without the strong support of Mr Alan Harrison of Warwick Business School. He has not only encouraged me to publish the book, but also compiled my draft, checked and rewritten it. Professor Sasaki of the Graduate School of Systems Management at the University of Tsukuba and Professor Emeritus Kondo of Kyoto University has also kindly advised me and looked over the draft. I would also like to acknowledge Mr and Mrs Teruhisa Yuasa's encouragement to publish an account of my experience. Finally, I would like to thank all our company members including my colleagues Mr Kojiri and Mr Enoki as well as Yuasa Sales Company members who have given good support to this company and the many British people, including the EETPU, local council at Ebbw Vale, the Welsh Development Agency, the Welsh Office and the British Government, who have supported me and given me the opportunity to enjoy the beautiful country of Wales; as well as my wife and three children, some of whom had to live on their own in Japan during my seven and a half years' secondment.

Introduction

Yuasa Battery Company Limited is one of the world's largest and most diversified manufacturers of power source products. Based at Osaka in Japan, Yuasa develops, manufactures and sells a broad line of top-quality and high-performance automotive, industrial and consumer batteries. These include a wide range from lead-acid automotive, motor cycle, and nickel-cadmium batteries to stand-by and motive power as well as industrial power systems. Sales of lead-acid batteries account for just over 70 per cent of Yuasa's net sales, which in 1989 totalled ¥76 billion (£316 million). Sales from group subsidiaries and affiliates, and also from the overseas group mean that total sales amount to ¥140 billion. During its seventieth anniversary year in 1988, Yuasa launched its 13-year plan, entitled 'The New Great Prosperity'. The plan envisages growth of net sales for Yuasa battery to ¥200 billion by the year 2000, and a sales target for the battery group of ¥500 billion. Total group sales, including the Yuasa Shoji sister trading company, will be ¥1 500 billion. In his vision for the twenty-first century, Yuasa President Mr Teruhisa Yuasa commented:

> In the business realm, industries are rapidly diversifying and reorganising. Thus to survive, companies will have to adjust to the advances in production methods, technology, information, internationalisation and also to an increasingly sophisticated and diverse consumer profile. To tackle such challenges of the coming century, Yuasa Battery stresses above all creativity. My vision of Yuasa is of an active and creative company that promotes innovation and also integration with the increasingly close-knit world community. In these ways I hope that Yuasa can live up to its motto:

> 'Toward contributing to the richness of humanity and the world through the attainment of a creative enterprise group'.

Decision to set up Yuasa Battery (UK) Limited

Establishment of a battery sales company in the UK in March 1981 was followed six months later by the decision to build a plant in Wales in order to meet the increasing demand for sealed, small-sized lead-acid batteries for applications such as computer back-up and security in Europe. The decision to set up a manufacturing base had some unusual features. The establishment of manufacturing subsidiaries in the UK in recent years has mainly been a story of how to beat existing trade barriers and to gain easier access to Europe. Yuasa Battery (UK) Limited therefore has something of a unique experience in establishing a manufacturing plant in Wales because the products that it makes are not subject to the same form of import limitations as other electrical goods. This means that the UK company has only a small advantage over Japanese-based companies in cost terms. The challenge for the new factory was to maintain cost competitiveness with Japanese-based companies while building on the advantages of its European-based location. While there are manufacturing competitors in the US and in Germany, the main competitors for these products are Japanese manufacturers based in Japan.

Selection of Ebbw Vale site

Yuasa had little doubt that the UK would be the best place for its European manufacturing base. UK culture and technologies had become very familiar to the Japanese. Preliminary studies were carried out on industrial sites in the UK. Although the Ebbw Vale area was industrially very depressed, it had many young people of working age and good assistance from the Welsh Office in terms of well organized consulting advice and financial subsidy. Although potential employees were often not well trained or experienced, we were confident that it would be possible to develop good people by on-the-job training.

With the benefit of several years' experience, we can now say that our choice has proved to be a very good one and that we have enjoyed working with the pleasant and friendly people here. Another bonus has been living in this very beautiful country. It is just fifteen minutes' drive from Ebbw Vale to Brecon Beacon National Park, which I think is one of the nicest spots in the world.

Company outline

Landmarks in the development of Yuasa Battery (UK) Limited are summarized in Table I.1.

Financial performance of the company has been good. It was starting to make a monthly profit after one year's operation, and covered all loses after two years. After three years it had returned all loans and started on a tripling of capacity. The sales turnover trend since start-up is shown in Figure I.1.

After six years the plant was further expanded to allow complete production from raw material to assembly. Within its product range, the company now enjoys a 60 per cent market share in the UK and nearly 30 per cent of the European market As a result it now has a great advantage over its Japanese-based competitors.

Table I.1 Landmarks for Yuasa Battery (UK) Ltd

Oct 81	Establishment of Yuasa Battery (UK) Ltd
	Construction of Factory 1 starts
June 82	Training started on site
Oct 82	Production start-up on 1 Oct
Oct 83	Company moves into profitability
Oct 84	All accumulated losses paid back
Oct 85	Positive cash-flow; all loans paid back.
	Decision taken to triple capacity
Apr 86	Yuasa wins Queen's Award for Export
Oct 86	Factory 2 starts up, tripling capacity
June 87	QC presentations to Duke of Gloucester
Oct 88	Production volumes now 10 times first year.
	Factory 3 starts up, adding injection moulding capability
Oct 89	Company members 480
	Local raw materials content 90%
	UK market share 60%
	60% of sales exported to continental Europe
	Output: 200 000 batteries/month

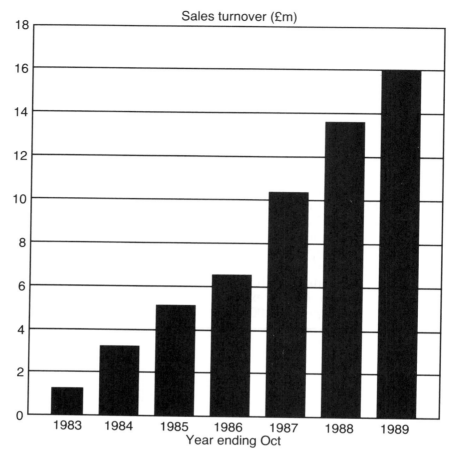

Figure I.1   Sales turnover (£ million).

1 SETTING OUT TO COMPETE WITH JAPAN

And so, in October of 1981, three Japanese employees of Yuasa of Japan arrived in the UK to establish the new company. The factory was being built on a new industrial estate at Ebbw Vale in north Gwent. The weather that winter turned extremely cold and snowy, and it proved difficult to arrange simple things such as the installation of telephones and the delivery of desks. Recruitment was also a problem, for there were days when it was extremely difficult to reach the factory, although such problems did not stop some enthusiastic applicants who walked miles to attend interviews. Needless to say, their determination impressed us, and indeed most of those intrepid applicants are still with the Company.

In those early days, I reflected on the task that lay ahead. In 1981, the European market was dominated by Japanese products made in Japan. Price competition for the sealed lead-acid battery was intense, leaving little room for a European-based newcomer to enter the market, even though components are easily available domestically. No special duties or volume restrictions applied to the export of these products from Japan to Europe, so the cost advantage of establishing a manufacturing company in Europe was only 7 to 8 per cent. Such a small differential was easily absorbed by Japanese companies in general, so that competing with European-based companies under these conditions was not a problem. As a result, our new company had to compete directly against Japanese-based companies on virtually equal grounds.

Devising a strategy to win

Setting a plan to ensure that the new company could compete against the established companies was very difficult. My simple targets to overcome the problems were as follows:

- To set quality levels equal to or better than Japanese quality levels.
- To attain Japanese productivity levels.
- To establish three-shift operation.

Since Japanese companies normally use only one or two shifts working in assembly, our company would have an advantage providing the first two criteria were met. If we could achieve all three of these simple targets, I could foresee that the company would make money without even seeing the profit/loss account!

Policy for making an excellent company

As a British company Yuasa Battery (UK) Limited needed to compete directly with Japanese companies. To achieve this a new management system had to be created. The new system would not be purely Japanese-style management, but one that could compete effectively against the Japanese way. The need for this was apparent given the environmental, historical and cultural differences between Japan and the UK. In coming up with a new approach, it was perhaps fortunate that I was an ex-research and development (R&D) man and had no experience of Japanese manufacturing! My conclusion was as follows:

> Let's create the best management system to fit this company and sort out problems by seeking the best way as in a business school.

It was an ideal opportunity to introduce good ideas from companies around the world and to create a management style that best suited the location and objectives of our new company. It was a great challenge to start with a blank canvas and to paint a picture in our own way.

The UK industrial environment

As part of the preparation for the creation of our new management system, I started to observe working practices of companies in the UK. Some of these practices would not be wanted in the establishment of our new system. Typical of the things which made an impression on me were the following:

- When I visited company A close to lunch time, I noticed a queue of people in front of the canteen who were waiting for the lunch bell to ring. They could not enter the canteen, but had stopped work.
- On the production line in company B, a very simple reject which had been found by the inspector was passed to an operator who was not part of the production line for rectification. There seemed to be obvious demarcation.
- I watched pipe-laying work taking place outside our factory. Two men had dug up the road and then had to wait for the pipe-layers to arrive and complete their task before re-filling the hole. Pipe-layers and road diggers were independent of each other.
- Several companies on our industrial estate have collapsed. One company next door to us disappeared suddenly one night, removing all the machines at the same time.

It was obvious that when setting up the new company we should avoid such problems by establishing flexible working practices, responsibility for problems and discipline.

On the other hand, I found some small private businesses operating very efficiently. People in small engineering firms and family shops were working with great efficiency and for very long hours. Company members were very flexible according to the situation and there was a marked absence of demarcation. They got the job done by finding out the most efficient way of doing it. I also found that British people enjoy do-it-yourself more than their Japanese counterparts and had developed very good skills: for example, installing a new kitchen or even building an extension on their house. Britain once had a very strong tradition of craftsmanship, which we can still see today in beautiful Georgian and Victorian furniture. Although Britain seems to have lost those traditions, one can still find people retaining a sense of craftsmanship in the way that they maintain their classic car, make furniture by hand or lay out a beautiful garden. People can often show very high skills when they are interested in what they are doing. I thought that some people had simply lost interest in their job in industry. From the sixteenth century to the industrial revolution, people would have been much more excited about the prospects of working in industry.

How to get that excitement back into the job in industry has seemed to me the key point of my work. This cannot be achieved in the old ways, but by a different way which fits into the industrial environment of the locality.

Advantages of Japanese industry

From my early observations the Japanese industrial environment appeared to enjoy three major advantages in attitude towards work over the British:

- The majority of Japanese workers committed themselves fully to a full day's work.
- The majority of Japanese workers adhered strictly to company rules and procedures.
- The majority of Japanese workers strived to improve.

To compete with these advantages is not so easy. In contrast, the attitude of many British people in the early 1980s was as follows:

- Just work for the money. 'I will produce a given amount but no more.'
- Although there are often company rules, they are not followed and the enforcement of them is not strict.
- Improvement in working practices and productivity is not my business but should be left to the experts.

To compete effectively with Japan, we would have to break such bad habits and create similar attitudes to those prevalent in Japan. Such positive attitudes must become everyday behaviour for my new company and not be forced. But how could we realize such goals? To begin with, it was not clear to me how this would be achieved in a British environment.

The importance of improvement

There seems to be a difference in attitude to selling price and manufacturing cost between Japanese and British companies. In Japan, manufacturing people have become accustomed to thinking that the selling price is coming down every year, but in Britain many companies think that the selling price can be increased every year. Typically customers are notified of this by a letter which states that the reason for prices going up is wage and material cost increases. The best British companies do not think this way, but many traditional companies have disappeared as a result of this kind of attitude. As a result of such an attitude, customers gradually leave the supplier and find a better one. When this happens, it is the start of a vicious cycle of cost increases as the volume of sales declines.

Of course every year many individual costs do increase: for example, there may be salary increases, material cost increases, or maintenance cost increases due to machine deterioration. The same applies in the office. There is a physical limitation to the speed at which you can type, and to the speed you can speak on the telephone (Figure 1.1)! There is only one way to counteract these problems, and that is improvement and creative activities. While physical work is always limited, creative work has no limitations. So the effect of material cost increases can be wiped out by reducing scrap and waste, and by design improvements. The cost of machine maintenance can be reduced by prevention and by improvement work. In the office, ideas for improvement can reduce both paperwork and the number of telephone calls. If people do not try to improve by saying that they are too busy doing routine work, then problems will not only continue but they will generate other problems and costs will escalate. Everybody in the company must be involved in improvement activities. If such activities are limited to only part of the company then only part of the problems will be sorted out.

Figure 1.1   There's a physical limit to the amount of work you can do!

To avoid the vicious cycle of cost increases, each section should list all the problems which affect the work they do. Once these have been put in order, from the easiest to the most difficult, they can be allocated to team members one by one, depending on the individual's ability. When everybody in the company is engaged in such improvement activities, the company's problems will be reduced faster and faster. Imagine two companies A and B who are competing with each other:

- Company A puts all its efforts into sorting out existing routine problems.
- Company B stresses the importance of improvement and the elimination of problems.

If you compare the costs of these two companies, you will find a big difference after two to three years.

The keys to success

There are just two fundamental factors for success in business:

- increasing the individual output of all company members;
- ensuring that the company advances in the correct direction for the future.

The second factor is clearly the responsibility of top management. It reflects the business aims of the company and therefore should be clear enough to be understood by all company members.

In competing with Japanese companies, it is the first factor which appears to provide European companies with the greatest difficulties. It is like racing a car: the power output of the engine is being continuously increased and the parts are gradually uprated as they respond better and better to the excellent driver of top management.

In Japan the majority of companies are engaged in quality control (QC) circle activities or similar. Many European companies have attempted to organize QC circles but have, with few notable exceptions, failed. Japanese culture and environment over the past 40 years have uniquely supported the development of QC circles. Lack of understanding in the UK was brought home to me when one of our circles presented results of their activities to a local business forum. Most of the questions after the presentation were directed at how much money our people had received for their ideas. If the concept of work is only in terms of monetary reward, it is very difficult to promote QC circle activities. In Japan, people often think that increasing ability is more important than increasing output of work. If we can increase our trainees' abilities, then in the long term we will be able to expect more output from them.

The basis of Japanese success

After the Second World War, Japan experienced a very different industrial environment, which is compared with the Western environment in Figure 1.2.

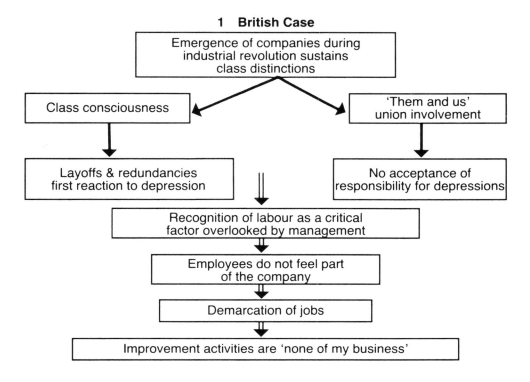

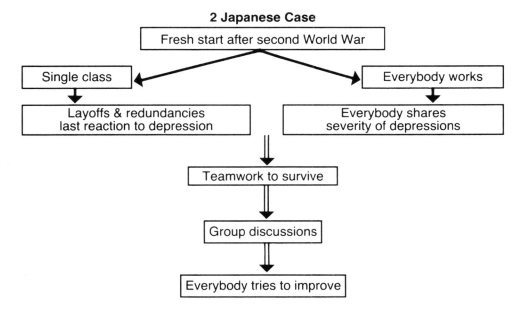

Figure 1.2.   Development of attitudes to work

During the 30 years for which I have worked for Yuasa the company, like many others, has been faced with several business downturns. During those difficult times we did more to save room lighting and used pencils with caps after they had become too short to use. Although they were small measures in themselves, such thinking gradually spread through the factory as well, and our operators came up with more ideas to save water, electricity, materials and so on. This is the background to the way QC circle activities started off. Because of the lifetime employment system in Japan, company members were not afraid to come up with ideas for improving their jobs, and so took an active interest in the improvement of costs and quality. The younger Japanese generation has not shared the hard experiences that followed the Second World War, and therefore QC circle activities will become more difficult to promote. However, in Europe, lay-offs and redundancies are the first remedy to be taken by a company which is facing a depression. This is the easy way for top management; they seem to find it too difficult to survive by promoting team activities to save money and improve methods. If a company handles the employee in the same way that it handles a component, then the employee's attitude will be one of working only for money.

Competition

Competition provides a very good opportunity for improvement. Again it is the same as in sport, for without competition players are unable effectively to improve their abilities. Japanese companies did not originally set out to become number one in the world. They just tried to survive in the competitive home market in conditions of lifetime employment. To start with they simply fought against other competitors in Japan. But, one by one, companies started to look outside Japan and found that they were in a good position in relation to competitors world-wide.

The most important thing is to use competitive situations for improving your company. Face the competitors directly and improve the ability of all your company members to compete. Japanese companies faced many severe times in the past. Each time they overcame the effects of a depression they grew.

Over the past few years, the Japanese economy has provided a very comfortable environment for businesses. I think that this time in Japan will be reflected later as a turning-point for a new era with a lessening of economic strength. On the other hand, European industries are being forced to face greater competition as a result of the single market after 1992, which will no doubt strengthen European-based industries.

A different approach to increase individual output

Given the different circumstances in the UK, introduction of QC circles in the same way as in Japan would not work. The key point is to identify how we can ensure that everybody develops an interest in their work and so to let them develop the incentive for improving the total output of the company. Simply putting people into QC circles and asking them to put forward ideas in the Japanese way would not be sufficient. A different approach is needed, and it should be based on an understanding of how people are motivated. People in the UK are much more motivated by sports and hobbies than are their Japanese counterparts. There is a very wide scope which is available for individual interests to be served. If we could induce the same sense of interest in the work of individuals, then it would be possible to make an even better environment than is possible in Japan. While people work for money they are also using up the uncountable value of the eight hours a day that they are at work (Figures 1.3–1.5). It would be much better if people not only were paid for work but also enjoyed the eight hours of their life by taking the initiative in creative activities. Developing in an individual the level of commitment at work that he shows in sports and hobbies is the key point for success.

A modern approach to personnel and industrial relations

In the past personnel and industrial relations people were mainly concerned with recruitment and with trade union negotiations. This was basically reactive work, because they reacted when there was a shortage of people or some difficulties in industrial relations. The modern task for personnel and industrial relations people is more upstream work, that is, a greater concern with prevention and with positive improvement. For example, finding out who the good people are, and developing a good relationship with them, are more important than selection interviewing. Developing a sound industrial relations environment for everyday work is more important than high levels of skills in trade union negotiations. As industry evolves and company information systems become more widely accessible to company members, the methods for promoting good industrial relations should also evolve. However, the purpose of industrial relations in promoting the happiness and welfare of members remains constant and is a common purpose shared by company and trade union. The protection of company members from hazardous or dangerous work must be the priority of the company before it becomes a union matter. The company which ignores these matters shows a lack of sensitivity in coping with

Figure 1.3. *I'd much rather walk up a mountain, even if the pack's heavy and it's raining . . . than be asked to carry a lead ingot, even if it's sunny*

Figure 1.4. *Life is too precious to waste, so why did you waste your life when you were at work?*

Figure 1.5. *Work is boring, but sports and hobbies really make me come alive!*

a modern business. Top managers must feel a stronger responsibility for employee welfare than shop stewards, otherwise they will not be successful at increasing the individual output of company members.

Although computers and sophisticated machines form the popular concept of a modern business, the key competitive activities of selecting, systematizing, maintaining and improving these machines are still carried out by human beings. We formed a single union agreement with the electricians' union (EETPU) because it has an ability to understand these modern business trends. Good communications between company senior management and union representatives are vital. These parties must regularly confirm their responsibility for keeping company members in the best possible working conditions. We have been very pleased with our joint efforts with the EETPU in this area.

New management principles

In the new company, I installed two new management principles:

- We will create a new management style which best suits our company, by discussing management problems every day as is done in a business school, and by using good management practice from across the world adapted to suit this company.
- The main purpose of the new management style is to encourage all company members to have an interest in their work, to help them enjoy their work and to let them improve themselves.

As a result of these new principles, management will improve the overall company performance.

2 PERSONNEL POLICIES

It is not necessary to perform gymnastic exercises or to sing the company song in the morning, but if there are 'them and us' relations on the shop floor it will never be possible to increase individual output. Therefore 'them and us' relationships must first of all be destroyed. During the hard times after the Second World War Japanese people – who enjoyed lifetime employment – shared the severity of a company depression by saving material and improving productivity through teamwork. As a result they have unconsciously broken the 'them and us' relationship which they too had before the war. Breaking this relationship in the UK is a challenge for the culture and for the industrial history of the country. Many traditional union activities have sprung up over the years to address this area. Breaking the old habits is not an easy thing to do. It is not achieved simply by understanding the problem better. It is only gradually achieved as a result of everyday activities which break down the barriers.

Breaking bad habits

Breaking bad habits which have arisen as a result of traditional attitudes to work places the onus fairly and squarely on the management of the business. It is essential for senior people to be very disciplined in themselves and to set a good example. I view the process as one of continuous improvement, which is illustrated in Table 2.1. Further management initiatives aimed at breaking bad habits were as follows:

● The MD and staff cleaned the operators' locker room every day at the same time over a period of six years.

- The MD and staff toured the plant every day at the same time. In addition to communicating, the staff helped the operators by, for example, moving the material, cleaning the machines and picking up and moving components.
- Once a week at the same time, the MD made a morning speech to explain the philosophy and policy of the company, together with practical ways of realizing that policy.
- A morning meeting was held every day to allow people from all parts of the organization, including shop floor, personnel, accounts, maintenance and so on to discuss problems and actions.
- Thirty minutes' communication and discussion time was allowed at the beginning of each shift so that people knew the previous day's productivity and quality performance compared to the equivalent Japanese figures and so that they could develop ideas for improvement in QC circles.
- Wherever possible we operated a 'promote from within' policy to ensure that a subordinate's improvement and ability were rewarded.
- We ensured that people first showed that they were capable of carrying out a higher graded job before their level of pay was increased.

These initiatives are described in more detail later on.

Table 2.1   Breaking bad habits: A continuous cycle of improvement led by senior managers

---

1   Demonstrate a good practical example of the action that is wanted
2   Fully explain the purpose and effectiveness of the action
3   Repeat this explanation many times
4   Repeat the action with the subordinates doing it at the same time
5   While observing, let the subordinates carry out the action by themselves
6   Show appreciation to the subordinates if the action has been carried out correctly
7   Continue to observe the subordinates and let them continue
8   If there is a failure, repeat the cycle from step 1

Developing good people

Being described as 'a good company' means that you have many good people. Here the job of the managing director is simply to develop everyone into good people, and he or she will be appreciated according to the number of good people who have been developed in this way.

Similarly, the manager's job is to develop good people in his or her team. My definition of good people is well-disciplined and creative people.

If people can develop a vision of their job within the company along the lines of being number one operator in the world or being number one supervisor in the world, and if people try to get closer to such ideal visions by improving themselves, the company will no doubt become an excellent one. People must be motivated to want to become the best and not have to be told. I have heard that, in some Western industries, senior people sometimes hesitate to develop their subordinates because their position would be threatened. If senior people should think this way, I think that the problem lies in the system of evaluation of such people!

If senior people always evaluate subordinates on the results of their 'on-the-job training', the subordinates will be given the incentive to train their people in turn. One of the best methods of evaluation in the organization is to see what happens while the senior person is absent. If the section works well without the leader, then the leader must be working very well on training team members. So the evaluation of people at salary review time must include the results of training the team. Developing good people is the shortest route to making an excellent company in the long run.

Domestic promotion

Bad companies have historically managed their employees as components which gradually reduce in value and in cost performance. Excellent companies have always viewed their people as an asset which increases in value year by year. In this sense the job of the senior person in a good company is to improve subordinates. If the subordinates do improve themselves then they will have a chance to be promoted. Such a domestic promotion system provides a good incentive to all members, once they understand the system and its purpose.

For example, a vacancy for a welder can often be best filled by somebody who has no experience in that trade; this might be a person who is keen on sport, who enjoys car maintenance as a hobby, has many other interests and is keen on self-improvement, as well as being a good potential team leader. Such a person would have great potential to contribute to the company during his or her working life, and could learn welding very easily and do a good job. Bad companies tend to spend less care on recruiting the right people than they spend on investment in an expensive machine, even though the total investment in a person during their working life is far greater than investment in the machine.

A good company has a good culture. A good culture cannot be developed if people are constantly moving on. A person who is recruited from outside the company into senior management may not be able to adapt easily to the existing culture and sometimes a company recruits a mismatched person by mistake.

Improving people is not an easy thing to undertake, but a company which has the ability to improve its people by growing them from within is a company which has the ability to become an excellent one. All of our factory management are people who joined us as operators over the last six years, and who have been promoted from within. Such people were promoted primarily for their potential to develop further. This policy has led to continuity in the development of our company culture.

Rewarding ability

To encourage the company's infinite ability to improve, it is very important to break the bad habits of 'I only work for the money' as well as 'them and us'. If people only work for the rate for the job, then they will resist continuous improvement and fail to become part of the overall company team.

In day-to-day work on the shop floor, people's conditions are changing all the time; for example, someone's performance may be affected because they have caught a cold, one person could be more or less experienced than another, someone else stronger or less strong. The manager's task is to achieve good team work in such a constantly changing environment. If managers can only think about the money they earn, they cannot manage their people who think in the same way. In an ideal production line the healthy operator must help the weaker operator and the experienced operator must help the less experienced operator. These are the sort of actions that teamwork demands in practice.

Jonathan Davies was a very successful rugby union player who dedicated himself to his sport. As a result he progressed from the amateur league at local level and played for Wales. Without this determined dedication, his natural talents would probably not have developed to such a degree. It was only after he had shown this attitude that he achieved success and was able to gain financial reward for his efforts by turning to professional rugby.

It is the same in business: if people keep thinking about the money they are paid and that they gain nothing by working hard, they will not be able to improve themselves and to enjoy their life at work. Life is very tedious if you work for money only and so the quality of working life is very poor.

In general it is difficult to improve someone's ability simply by changing their job or their salary. Ability is improved as a result of the individual's everyday efforts. We developed three principles for rewarding ability:

● Implement an in-house promotion system.
● Improve ability first and the money will follow.
● Senior people must monitor their subordinates' effort and improvement in ability.

So we do not advertise opportunities for promotion in our company; it is the senior person's job to keep track of people's abilities. The promotion of all senior line people and managers from within the company has demonstrated that effort would be rewarded and has gone a long way to encouraging people to show their ability and improve first before expecting reward. A senior hand is expected to work for three months in that position without receiving any more pay than when he or she was an operator. A supervisor must work for six months without additional payment.

This not only proves that the person promoted to a new job has the ability to do it, but also ensures that people realize that they should be prepared to do other duties and to take on responsibilities when the necessity arises. I learned the principle when a supervisor was forced to be away from work for a long period of time. His senior hand filled the position for three months without once complaining. During this time he demonstrated his ability and also gained a lot of respect from his fellow workers. His achievement was rewarded when he was officially promoted to the position of supervisor and given a special bonus payment.

Productivity bonus system

We installed a productivity bonus system for each process in each shift. Bonus was earned by comparing productivity achieved with the equivalent process in the Japanese parent. The cost of scrap is removed from the output. Consequently people try to prevent scrap from arising and, if for some reason the shift is overmanned, surplus people will be released to another section to maintain a high level of productivity. The calculation is very strict. Any problems which could affect productivity, such as machine breakdowns, technical problems or component problems, are not excluded from the productivity calculation. The only exception to this rule is a power cut, which is considered to be *force majeure*. Bonus calculations are carried out separately for all nine unit business groups in the company. Bonus at salary review time is determined in proportion to the productivity index.

By always relating the productivity bonus to Japanese levels, we ensure that continuous improvement is built into the bonus system. This distinguishes our system from measured day work, where the same standards may be in use for many years and may have become quite out of date with current practice. Further, such a system provides no incentive for the operator to improve (other than to gain more idle time!).

Self-improvement mechanism

Ideally individuals and sections should improve themselves positively every day without being asked to do so. But to start off with it is very difficult in practice because people just do not have any real improvement experience. The right environment for continuing improvement can be obtained if people have sufficient experience to break through a threshold. We had some ideas for achieving this:

- Give everyone repeated training of the improvement mechanism described in Chapter 3. Ensure that each trainee understands the mechanism completely.
- Ensure that each person has a good understanding of the difference between the present situation and what could be achieved ideally. Let the trainee understand what are the problem points in relation to the job and in relation to his or her work.
- Experiencing the enjoyment of achieving success in making improvements creates energy to achieve more.

Introduction of 'Just-in-Time'* production systems within the factory creates excitement automatically! Because buffer stocks have been run down or eliminated, a problem in a process immediately becomes a problem for the factory as a whole.

Selection interviewing

As I have said before, a good business depends on the quality of its people. Every manager would agree with this statement, but not so many are eager to recruit the most suitable people for the long-term good of the company. As a result, many managers recruit people without taking proper care over their selection. It may be that they think they can change people easily. But a random assembly of people cannot develop the required culture of the company: without an appropriate

*For definition of Just-in-Time, see the glossary on p.83.

culture, a company cannot exist in a stable form. Company culture is the evidence of the quality of creative teamwork.

Whether you view people as components or as assets for the future makes a lot of difference in the approach to the selection interview.

- If you view a person as a component, you are interested in present ability.
- If you view a person as an asset, you will be interested in future potential much more than present ability.

The asset value of a machine will decrease year by year, but the asset value of a good person will increase in time. In this sense, the recruitment of people from operators to management must be done very carefully indeed.

If we want to recruit two operators in our company, four applicants are interviewed by the management, including the supervisor of the section. The four applicants will have been selected in advance by the personnel people from eight applicants, and those eight applicants will have been selected from sixteen application forms. In fact it was often found that people can be better selected by supervisors than by personnel people.

For the first five years, I interviewed all applicants personally. At first, my English was not so good and I could not understand all that the applicants were saying, but I could observe their personality and could make some fairly accurate points as a result. My own involvement always helped to demonstrate that I think that people are very important.

From the beginning I greeted each 'freshman' on their first day at work by shaking hands and saying to them: 'Welcome to Yuasa, please enjoy your life through Yuasa' (Figure 2.1). At first, people could not understand at all why I did this, but gradually they came to realize what I was trying to do through my attitude and policy.

Training

On-the-job training is better than off-the-job. The senior person's task is to develop good subordinates by recognizing that the full eight hours of every working day are training time. During training, the most important points to emphasize will be taking the lead in solving problems and taking the lead in improvements. If as a result all members become well disciplined and creative the company will become stronger and stronger.

At the beginning of on-the-job training we notice that the only thing trainees gain is self-satisfaction. So the senior person must set a somewhat higher target and then check whether the trainee is doing 'a little better every day'.

Figure 2.1 Each 'freshman' was welcomed personally to the company by the MD

3   IMPROVEMENT

In Chapter 1 I stated that increasing individual output was the more difficult to achieve of the keys to success. It means that everybody is engaged in improvement activities. Operators try to improve themselves and the work they do through QC circle activity. Staff people must likewise engage in improvement activities: it would be quite wrong if they only kept to a routine, systematized job.

The more senior you are, the more time you must devote to improvement activities aimed at making an excellent company, otherwise you cannot survive in the hard business world. The scope of improvement activities will depend on the level within the organization. Junior people are limited to factors which surround the job they do. Senior managers should seek to improve the systems and work environment of the company as a whole. The aim should be to systematize routine work and to replace it by robot or computer so that people can be freed to work on the next level of improvement of company systems and procedures. The changes involved are illustrated in Figure 3.1. Improvement is a creative activity which enables people to enjoy and find satisfaction in the world of work.

Improvement is enjoyment

To be able to measure your improvement in any field is very fulfilling. This applies equally to sports such as rugby or running, to learning languages and to the ability to solve problems. You can measure your improvement at golf very easily by comparing your scores for different rounds over a period of time. Similarly, enjoyment can be gained by observing growth in other people, particularly those close to you who have benefited from your own advice and training. The most fulfilling thing for the coach of a rugby team is to see his players grow and improve their skill. And it is the same in work, where improvement in your subordinates can be an enjoyable thing for you. Once people have had experience of their own improvement, they can share in the

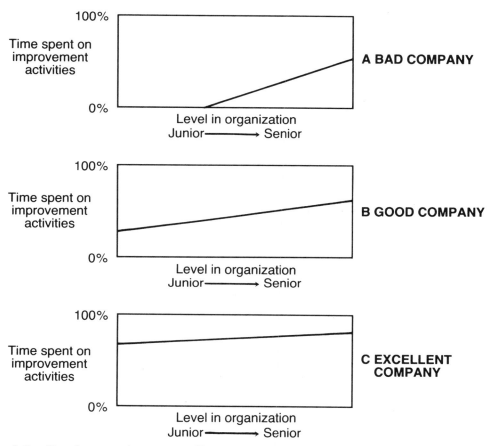

Figure 3.1 Development into an excellent company: percentage of time spent on improvement activities at all levels

enjoyment of the continual process of improvement. But if they have not shared such an experience, it can be difficult for them to understand and it can be difficult for them to be persuaded that they should improve. So in order to start off it is better to choose apparently small duties, such as filing, reporting methods and even saying, 'good morning' in a friendly way to improve human relations. Through such activities people will come to understand that the intention to achieve better things is the essence of improvement and self-improvement.

QC circle activity

It is very difficult consistently to maintain high quality on assembly production work, especially on a three-shift pattern. There has to be a dependence on the operator's manual skills, which in turn depend on the attitude and thinking of the operator. If the operator is interested in the job, it is possible to concentrate on the manual work. Otherwise it would be possible to miss a small point which could lead to vital defects. How to generate an interest in work is the key point in achieving success. If operators have an interest in their work, then it is possible for them to enjoy that portion of their life as they should. It was for these reasons that I started QC circle activities right from the beginning. The first half-hour of every shift was dedicated to communication and QC circles. The shift supervisor reported on the previous day's productivity and quality results compared with Japan and with the other shifts. The remainder of the period was devoted to QC circle activities, with small groups discussing possible improvement projects. All operators were taught how to use a 'fish-bone chart'* to analyse problems affecting the work they do. The use of such methods helped to create a methodical and consistent form of analysis and enabled everyone to take part in solving problems.

To begin with, not all members could understand what to do and some complained that the 30 minutes was time lost, using it only to complain about their working conditions to the managers. But we can now look back on this system over the last six and a half years with a sense of achievement. QC circles have been encouraged in every possible way, until now we have over 70 groups who have produced more than three thousand ideas for improvement. During the last three years we have sent QC circle representatives to Japan to present their ideas at Yuasa group seminars which are attended by Yuasa top management. We also took the opportunity for our operators to present their ideas to the Duke of Gloucester during the opening ceremony of our new factory. QC circle development has taken place in five main stages, as follows.

First stage: initial training   Although we had no QC circle experts within the company, I was an ex-R&D man and had developed my own experience in applying for around 150 patents. This had helped me to know the process of researching facts and creating new ideas and to acquire a great taste for the enjoyment that this process can bring. I wanted to impart some of this enjoyment to other company members and so to lead them to realize that their working hours could become more satisfying if they participated in QC circle activities.

Fish-bone charts are a very convenient way to involve everybody in problem solving, and I started to train our people in their use. It is boring to take a serious subject from the beginning, so initially we used everyday examples such as 'successful dating' and 'how to win the next rugby match'. People enjoyed these discussions and at the same time

*For definitions of QC Circle and Fish-bone chart, see the Glossary on p.83

learned about using fish-bone charts. Then we moved on to the more serious examples of problems which they found on the assembly line. In order to make training more enjoyable for our new employees, I came up with the idea of appointing a personable lady member of our staff to become the first contact that our new employees have with QC circle activities during their initial induction to the company (Figure 3.2). So I trained a lady who was working in the laboratory to become a trainer in addition to her normal job. She has done very well at this task.

Figure 3.2 Training in the use of fish-bone charts

Second stage: appreciation at site

In the early days of circle activity I found that many groups were jumping to ideas without the use of my systematic approach using fish-bone charts. I felt that it was more important for them to enjoy the success of installing new ideas than for me to insist that fish-bone charts were used, and allowed people to install ideas by themselves without evaluation. When installation had been completed, I went down to the shop floor and took a photograph of the installed ideas, along with the group responsible, and published the photographs for all to see in our canteen (Figure 3.3). So successful was this that we had very soon covered one complete wall. A visiting delegation from the Union of Japanese Scientists and Engineers was moved to comment that this was 'indeed the origin of QC circles, and people are really enjoying them'.

Figure 3.3   Photographs of installed ideas on the wall of the canteen

Third stage: presentation In Japan there are many opportunities to present the work of QC circles by means of presentations and competitions at factory, local and national levels. These events have helped companies and individuals to learn from each other.

There is a shortage of such events in the UK, so initially we used every opportunity to encourage our people to be proud of their achievements and to take pleasure in presenting them to important visitors (Figure 3.4). One such opportunity came when we won the Queen's Award for Export. Our people presented their ideas to the Secretary of State for Wales, Mr Nicholas Edwards (Figure 3.5). The operators who were going to present rehearsed many times before the ceremony and became very excited about it! Their presentation went very well and was very much enjoyed by the 150 guests. The presenters

Figure 3.4 *Every opportunity was used to enable QC circles to make presentations of their work*

Figure 3.5 *QC circle presentation to the Secretary of State for Wales, Mr Nicholas Edwards, together with (right) Mr Yuichi Yuasa, the former chairman of Yuasa Battery Co Ltd*

were also delighted to see the reaction of our guests and were proud of their activity. A further opportunity came later at the opening ceremony of our expanded factory which was attended by HRH Duke of Gloucester and the Lord Lieutenant, Mr Hanbury Tenison.

Fourth stage: Yuasa competition

As more people became proficient in public presentations we decided to hold our own internal competition each year. Every three months, the top ten ideas are selected for a simple presentation to a panel of judges consisting of management, staff and shop floor. From each quarterly round the best two ideas are selected for the final round of the best eight entries. Teams are encouraged to present their ideas to best effect by using slides, video and so on. The best project is selected and the team goes to Japan for the annual Yuasa competition.

Fifth stage: line presentation

To create further opportunities for operators to make presentations, we came up with the idea of presenting displays on the shop floor, where visitors can be shown projects at short notice by a member of the responsible group using a presentation mounted on a board. Visitors are always pleased to see these presentations and listen seriously to the operator's explanation. Although they initially felt very shy, operators now enjoy making these presentations, which provide further incentive and pride (Figure 3.6).

Figure 3.6   Circle members explaining their project to a group of visitors

The point of promoting the QC circle activities has been to make work time more enjoyable by involving everybody in the improvement of product quality and the work environment and also to give people the opportunity to display their success in these activities.

The mechanism of improvement

After 20 years' experience in R&D, I felt that I understood the mechanism of invention pretty well. In my view the fundamental principle of invention is similar to QC circle improvement activities, and I used these principles to train our people. The mechanism we used is shown in Table 3.1. This mechanism was displayed on the wall of our meeting room and served to remind us always to take precise and logical steps in any problem-solving activity. Many people remarked that they had been using a similar process, but usually unconsciously. This often meant that some of the stages were jumped, which usually makes the problem-solving process less effective. By defining the mechanism of improvement, people are helped to know what part of the improvement process they are discussing and therefore to concentrate on that part. Sometimes people just discuss the facts related to a problem, and do not proceed further. In another case, they may analyse the facts and make a graph but do not go any further, as if they had achieved their work. Very often an idea will be installed but there is no check on the eventual result or ensuring that a new system has been adhered to. Therefore it is important to emphasize that every step must be taken in a logical sequence and that the whole process is repeated if necessary.

Table 3.1   Stages in problem solving.

---

1 Know the facts
  the precise facts about the problem to be solved
2 Analyse the facts
  using fish-bone charts helps here
3 Identify the key point
  finding the basic cause of the problem
4 Generate ideas
  for the most efficient way to solve the problem
5 Develop the idea
  refine the ideas and develop them into a practical design
6 Install the idea
  put the solution into practice
7 Check the result
  if not enough, return to stage 1

The failure of improvement

As we have said above, making improvements is not easy and many failures can be attributed to failure to follow the mechanism shown in Table 3.1 in a systematic way. If you have not succeeded in cracking a problem, find out in which stage of the process you have failed.

You cannot come up with good improvements unless you have started out with the correct observations. If the data are incorrect, your computer analysis is rubbish. You should be prepared to improve your installed ideas the very next day. Refining the process of each improvement is also very important. This refining process means repeating the whole mechanism, starting with observation.

Many staff people think that recording data is an improvement in itself. In fact, it is only the first stage of problem solving. Staff people also must understand the process of improvement, so they too must engage in improvement activities and pursue the solution through to improved results on the production line.

No excuses

Excuses are a waste of time in solving problems. I never allowed managers to make excuses to me and after a few years managers and staff tried to avoid excuses when they talked to me because I always jumped on them. In turn, managers and staff pass on this habit to their subordinates, so helping the key point of the problem to be identified earlier and problems to be sorted out more quickly.

At the beginning of our operations, when I asked people why there had been a delay in getting something done, their reply was always along the lines of 'yes, but I asked A to do it, and he hasn't finished yet' or 'yes, I asked an outside company to send this repair component, but they can't supply us yet.' In other words, they were saying that, although they had promised me that the task would be completed, they had instructed somebody else who had not achieved the task in time – in other words, 'I am not wrong, it is somebody else or another company who is at fault.'

In such cases I always reacted by saying, 'Promising that you are going to do something means doing it. If your job is simply to transfer my instructions to your subordinate, you are not a manager but only a messenger boy. You must know the ability of the subordinate concerned, and if that person does not have the ability to achieve what you want you must get in there and help. That means you must have the ability to know what your subordinate is capable of, you must have the ability to evaluate work and you must have the ability to help the subordinate. That is the manager's job.'

In the same way, people must evaluate people or companies outside the organization and, if they have not been reliable in the past, we must instruct them sufficiently in advance to allow them to keep their promise on time. By avoiding excuses we can discuss positively the key point of the problem and so sort it out.

While I have prohibited the use of excuses which seek to blame others for failure to perform on time, I accept a notice of delay in advance of the promised date. This is because, if people approach me in advance and tell me what their problem is, then this is evidence that they are taking the task seriously. Now it is my turn to help them to create ideas to sort out the problems which prevent the promised date from being achieved.

Sensitivity

In modern business everybody must be engaged in creative activities. This applies whether you happen to be the operator, the accountant or the MD. Routine work will be taken over by robot or computer.

What then will remain for the human being in the business of the future? Only improvement. Once an aspect of work has been computerized, better systems can always be found, so computerization extends further. It is an infinite process. As I showed in the 'improvement mechanism' above, the process of improvement always begins by knowing the facts. This means that it requires sensitivity to find the problem. So another major spin-off for QC circle activities is their importance in improving an individual's sensitivity.

If people work like a machne, they will be replaced by a machine once the technology has been developed by the engineers. Alternatively their company loses out to competitors who are staffed by thinking people. Either way they will lose their job eventually. But if the operator has well developed sensitivities and so can detect small problems (such as noise, vibration and distortion) in advance of a major breakdown and so prevent it from happening, he or she is well equipped to work with automatic machines however sophisticated they may become. A highly automated machine is still a machine which requires proper maintenance and improvement.

So, if it has enough money, any company in any country can buy modern automatic machines. But the company will not be able to operate the machines efficiently without a similar investment in operators who have sensitivity and interest in these machines. People cannot be trained in such things in a short time. They result from the accumulation of everyday improvement activities.

I often explained the need for sensitivity in morning speeches as follows: 'If a manufacturing line operates in such a way that materials and components are the same, machines and jigs are the same, and process standards do not vary, then all batteries will be the same and we don't need either to check them or to have inspection equipment.'

In practice, however, we as human beings, miss the differences every day. It is very important to keep our shortcomings in mind and to try to become more sensitive in detecting differences in colour, odour, shape, sound and so on before we measure our work and record those measurements on a control chart.

4 COMMUNICATION

Communication is basic to the development of an excellent company. Human beings can create new ideas by bringing together information they learned in the past. If you do not know something, you cannot do it! It is like a computer: it will not do anything useful unless data have first been input. A creative company depends on information being shared by all company members. This does not mean that people who receive the same information do the same things with it. People must react differently to the information they receive. For example, a senior person should take a wider view than a subordinate, and use the information to take a longer-term perspective.

Only old-fashioned and inefficient management maintain their position by keeping information to themselves, keeping their subordinates in the dark. My company is the UK subsidiary of a Japanese multinational. If special meetings were frequently arranged by the Japanese members only, other company members would become suspicious and the trust in which the Japanese members are held would become vulnerable. To establish good communications, it is very important to make as much information as possible available to all company members so that team spirit extends even to those involved in routine activities. In my company the regular communication channels were weekly morning speeches, morning meetings, plant tours and the monthly advisory board. These are described in subsequent sections of this chapter. As a result of these company-wide communications, company members unconsciously share common information so that their involvement is stimulated and their understanding of each other's work is increased.

In this environment each company member tries to discharge their responsibility as a result of their own initiative taken to best fit each circumstance, and not by continually referring to the supervisor. For example, everybody was given information about forthcoming customer visits and individual groups prepared quality control circle presentations and technical presentations appropriate to the customer. Personnel people then prepared a welcome flag and board.

These preparations are systematically organized so that everybody is geared up to welcome the customer. The manager's task here is to communicate information effectively prior to the visit, to create a good atmosphere and to coordinate activities.

Communication on the shop floor

Improving communication between line and staff people is very important in improving factory efficiency. As long as staff people, like technical or maintenance and line people, simply complain about each other, we cannot progress as a company. This problem is often seen in the factory, where demarcation can be strong and inflexible.

In our company we have gone for overlapping responsibilities, as shown in Figure 4.1. If line people have a problem which needs staff help, that problem becomes the responsibility of the relevant staff section. If staff have a problem as a result of a line area, then the reverse applies. When a problem is found which is the responsibility of another section, you cannot simply complain to that section. But you can raise a clear problem point on the other section, inform your colleagues, and try to sort out the problem in cooperation with the other section. If the production line does not run well, for example, staff sections must recognize that something is wrong with their service support.

We developed three communication boards to help communication between line and maintenance people. These boards helped to classify whether the key point of the problem was a repair requirement, a prevention requirement or an improvement requirement. The terms 'repair', 'prevention' and 'improvement' are explained in Chapter 5 and the communication boards are illustrated in Figure 4.2.

If a production person notices a problem point which has occurred before (what we call a 'repeated' problem), it must be written on the prevention board and signed. The boards are displayed in the discussion room so that anybody can write down comments on them. Maintenance engineers check these boards once a day and allocate responsible people from inside or outside the factory to sort out the problems and enter target dates.

Multi-purpose plant tour

After the operator's locker room had been cleaned every morning, staff people engaged in a 'helping' plant tour which was aimed at helping production personnel. Staff people had to clear up rubbish from the shop floor and observe the production line and people from their individual professional point of view. This would include aspects such as health and safety, quality and technical points and maintenance. The

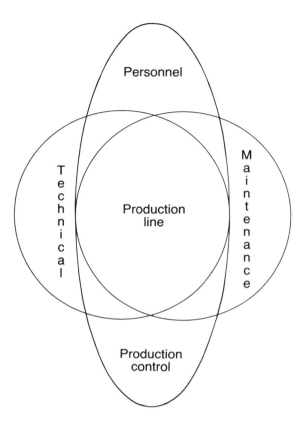

Figure 4.1   Overlapping responsibilities

rules of this 'helping plant tour' are that staff people must help things on the shop floor and observe problem points of the production process.

Sometimes I pushed batteries on a pallet from one process to the next, supplied components or cleaned lead waste from machines and equipment. I always wore the necessary protective equipment (mask and gloves) to enable me to carry out such helping duties. At each process I greeted the individual operator by saying, 'Good morning, how are you this morning?' (Figure 4.3). When I found an important problem, I called the relevant staff person over directly.

The plant tour lasted for around an hour. I could find out if shop floor people had some frustrating problem before they complained to me, and as a result I could discuss the problem with them and so could minimize their frustration. Greeting everyone and talking to them every morning made us feel more familiar with each other and respect each other better.

There was a very good reason for me to engage in such direct communication with shop floor people. When we started off our factory

REPAIR

No.	Casting	Pasting	Format'n	Assembly	Others	SUBJECT	DATE RAISED	PERSON RAISED	PERSON RESPONSIBLE	DATE / SIGN	TARGET/ FINISH DATE	IN OR OUT
1					✓	LEVEL GAUGE FOR 1·3 5·6 NOT WORKING	14/11	P. G. SHAREM	E. YOUNG.	E Young	30/11	IN
2				✓		SMALL COMPRESSOR, BATTERY WASHER	17/11	T. WILLIAMS	R. WEST	R West	21/11	OUT FLUID TECH.
3		✓				PASTE MIXER SAFETY SWITCHES	27/11	M. PARKER	E. YOUNG.	E Young	30/11	IN
4					✓	M&S INSPECTION GATE BROKEN	28/11	M. JONES	E. YOUNG	E Young	30/11	IN

PREVENTION

No.	Casting	Pasting	Format'n	Assembly	Others	SUBJECT	DATE RAISED	PERSON RAISED	PERSON RESPONSIBLE	DATE / SIGN	TARGET/ FINISH DATE	IN OR OUT
1			N° 2	✓		RENEW RUBBER SEALS ON 'L' LINE CHARGING BATH DOORS	9/3	T. WILLIAMS	R. WEST	R West	15/4	IN
2		✓	N° 1			CHANGE DRIVE BELT ROLLER	9/3	O. ENOKI	R. WEST	R West	26/3	IN
3				✓		NEW BUCKET ELEVATOR	15/3	T. GAIT	G. PRICE	G Price	31/5	OUT
4	✓					RENEW BRASS BLOCKS TIMING BELT	17/3	T. GAIT	R. WEST	R West	20/4	IN

IMPROVEMENT

No.	Casting	Pasting	Format'n	Assembly	Others	SUBJECT	DATE RAISED	PERSON RAISED	PERSON RESPONSIBLE	DATE / SIGN	TARGET/ FINISH DATE	IN OR OUT
1					✓	GUARDS REQUIRED AT U/SONIC AND ACID FILL	24/11	T. WILLIAMS	S. WARFIELD	S. Warfield	31/3	IN
2		✓				IMPROVED SCRAP CONVEYORS AT CUTTING M/C N.F	6/12	H. SESWICK	S. WARFIELD	S. Warfield	30/4	IN
3					✓	PUT BATH DOOR STOPS ON CHAINS	9/12	T. WILLIAMS	E. YOUNG.	E Young	30/3	IN
4					✓	TABLE SWITCH ON BURNER	14/12	C. PROTHEROE	E. YOUNG	E Young	30/1	IN

Figure 4.2   Examples of communication boards

Figure 4.3   Greeting individual operators on the multi-purpose plant tour

operations I asked supervisors to let me know what our operators' opinions were on a company event. While I got plenty of opinions from the supervisors, I later found out that they were not the operators' opinions at all, but the supervisors' alone. Now we do not have such problems any more, because if there is a miscommunication I find out about it on the plant tour! A further great benefit is that you can check up on the progress of projects and the implementation of decisions without relying on second-hand information alone.

Multi-communication meetings

When we started running the factory there were many teething problems. To sort out such problems it was necessary to ensure that people from all parts of the organization communicated and discussed things efficiently among themselves. To help encourage such communication I started short, informal meetings of senior members which were held every day. Meetings were informal in the sense that everyone stood in the room, and did not sit around the table. This meant that individuals could move from one small group to another to ensure that they made a contribution to a relevant problem. I also attended these meetings and listened in to the discussions. If the discussion was not along practical lines, or the ideas for sorting out the problems were unsound, I intervened and joined in the discussion to help. Such meetings helped to create a very flexible working atmosphere (Figure 4.4).

On one occasion, a shop floor process required a special small size of cloth for cleaning the product. But it was difficult to obtain such a small size of cloth in the time available. So we purchased large sheets and everybody at the standing meeting was issued with a pair of scissors and asked to cut the cloth. So while they were having their discussions during the standing meeting, everybody was busily cutting the cloth as well! It was amazing flexibility and continued for several weeks until a suitable supplier was found. Through such experiences we created an atmosphere whereby everybody had to help everybody else.

Figure 4.4   A multi-communication meeting

This method of conducting meetings proved to be a very successful means of communication, with all senior people being involved in discussing problems and available to other members for advice or help on a regular basis. Another benefit was that, as this meeting was established early on in the life of the company, members from different departments soon became familiar with each other. If we had set out with the more usual meeting format whereby everybody sits around a table and the discussions proceed according to an agenda, one subject after another, sectionalism might have developed and it would have been more difficult to develop flexibility within management.

300 morning speeches

During my time in the UK I gave a short speech every week to all managers, supervisors and senior hands – about 40 people in total. The purpose was to explain my policy and philosophy about management, the importance of improving the individual and the organization and the factors necessary to make an excellent company. This way, everybody would get to understand my everyday behaviour. In all, over 300 morning speeches of this nature, were made and were always written by me.

Figure 4.5 Delivering a morning speech

The key point of making these speeches was the development of an excellent company through the improvement of the individual members and the fulfilment of their working life. At the beginning of my morning speeches I often emphasized how important it is to have the right attitude towards improvement. My views are summed up by the motto:

'Intention and reflection make improvement.'

In fact, you will not achieve any target unless you have the intention to do so. On the other hand, you will achieve something in your life if you maintain a solid intention of achieving your set targets. By reflecting on your progess you could shorten the time that it takes you to achieve them. Every day should have a purpose. If you think that your work is reasonable, then you do not have reflection. Ask yourself:

'Can my work be improved in any way?'
'Is my attitude correct?'

It is necessary to learn from your activities in order to improve. Self-satisfaction is the enemy of improvement and slows down progress towards intended goals. Identifying the problem points is the first step in improvement. By reflecting on what you have achieved today and what you have failed to achieve, you are giving yourself a better opportunity to identify the problem points. Even in failure you must continue to succeed. After making a mistake, it is important to reflect on the improvement process. Reflection must be more than a recognition that something has gone wrong. Reflection must be striven for. Each situation must be run through in detail so that one can appreciate the problem and provide a solution. Creating pressure on yourself can cause deeper reflection. It is like getting fit: the more pressure you have on a regular basis, the more able you become to cope with pressure.

Advisory board

Every month, trade union and company representatives had a meeting to discuss collective matters to improve the welfare of members, information about company performance and ways of improving the company business information.

General office

Our general office allowed the MD, managers and staff to work together without any partitions (Figure 4.6). A natural reaction is for people to feel that they do not want to be exposed too much when they meet for the first time. But once you get to know each other very well you will find it is convenient to sit together in one room in the same way that you sit in your lounge at home with your family. Creating a good atmosphere like this pays dividends.

Apart from a few confidential matters, we have always communicated together in the general office. This has several advantages:

● People in the general office can share the same information.
● People get to know each other better.

GENERAL OFFICE

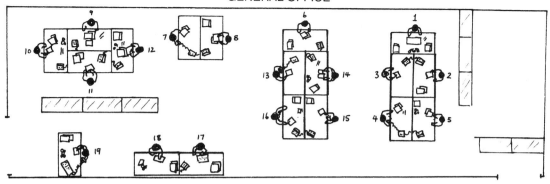

1. Managing Director	7. Personnel Manager	13. Injection Moulding Production Manager	17. Wages Clerk
2. Production Manager	8. Personnel Officer		18. Wages Clerk
3. Chief Engineer	9. Accounts Manager	14. Injection Moulding Technical Manager	19. Reception/Switch Board
4. Senior Engineer	10. Accountant		
5. Project Manager	11. Accounts Assistant	15. Technical Engineer	
6. Factory Manager	12. Accounts Clerk	16. Electrical Engineer	

Figure 4.6   The general office

● Senior people get to know the ability of their subordinates better and vice versa

Although it is not always necessary, in modern business it is better for company members to share the same information. Yet each company member will react in a different way. It is the same in a football game. Everybody must know where the ball is, yet each player moves differently according to his own intentions and ideas.

This is the ideal way for an organization to work in a modern business. The rules must be sound, but at each level of the company people must carry out their role, create good ideas and get good results. So once company members understand the principle and philosophy they can come to enjoy the general office system.

Communication through visual display

In our experience the best way to communicate is by visual display, with as little wording as possible. Too much writing will often lead to misunderstanding and certainly take more time to absorb. To use the advantages of visual display, we came up with several ideas, as indicated below.

Display room

One area of the factory was devoted to the display of information on company performance. The room was divided into compartments, as shown in Figure 4.7. Each compartment was the property of an individual section where up-to-date records of performance, such as production and productivity, reject levels and machine down-time

Figure 4.7   The display room: an example of communication by visual display

could be displayed. These records are displayed on large graphs or tables showing daily achievement against planned or targeted levels. The display room is open to any company member, who therefore has ready access to the current company situation.

Sample room
We set up a sample room in which we displayed all finished products and their component parts, including samples of defective or rejected items. We also included samples of our competitors' products. Again this area was open to anyone within the company to use, and was often a focus for QC circle activities.

Mottoes
Many improvement mottoes are displayed throughout the company, from shop floor to offices (Figure 4.8). We added a new motto every year. Historically, these included:

1982–3   'Quick Action'
    'A Little Better Every Day'
1984–5   'Prevention'
1986–7   'Improvement'
1988–9   'Creation and Efficiency'

Other mottoes that we came up with included:

'A tidy factory makes a tidy battery' (The word 'tidy' is used here in the Welsh sense of 'good looking').
'Ideas, Ideas, Ideas'

Figure 4.8   Mottoes displayed on large yellow cubes hanging from the roof of the factory

Above the sample room door is the motto

'Creativeness and Productivity'.

Simple wording   In all forms of communication the emphasis has been on simple and concise wording, with as much pictorial or graphical display as possible. The golden rules are:

● Do not write long sentences.
● One key point only for each display.
● Illustrate with a drawing wherever possible.

5 MAINTENANCE

Line people tend to think that problems which arise with the machines they use are the concern only of maintenance engineers. Difficulties with operating a machine are classified as 'maintenance problems' and by implication it is up to maintenance to sort them out. On the other hand, maintenance engineers often think that problems with machines are generally attributable to lack of care and attention by the operator. Both of these attitudes are examples of bad habits and lead to demarcation between the people involved. Unless there is cooperation between line and maintenance personnel, it becomes progressively impossible to maintain machines in good condition in the factory.

Do not accept complaints

We made it clear that all problems on the production line must at least be shared by line personnel. It is essential that operators do not wash their hands of problems which affect the work that they do, and blame the relevant service department. So operators are not allowed simply to complain to maintenance people about machine problems. However, they can raise clear problem points which concern their machines and ask maintenance personnel to improve those points.

To start off with it was unavoidable that such rules would lead to arguments on the shop floor. However, people on the shop floor gradually understood their responsibilities and started to take the initiative themselves to improve machine efficiencies by coordinating with relevant staff people. In order to take advantage of the improved opportunities of cooperation which such an attitude brings, shop floor management are now developing lists of problem points to discuss with the relevant staff people at the multi-communication meetings every day. Clearly the problem points raised can encompass issues other than maintenance, for example poor component quality. But it is interesting how maintenance issues have often helped to establish principles like this.

Looking at maintenance problems from the staff perspective, operating results should be evaluated by the number and extent of shop floor problems raised. The aim should be to improve machines, components, systems and so on before problems are raised by the shop floor people. Staff people's customers are the shop floor, so they must study the production line as their customer and make systems which help to ensure that the line works smoothly.

Furthermore, if an operator handles a machine roughly and damages it by operating it too quickly, the maintenance engineer must not complain to the operator. However, it is permitted to raise the problem point about operator movement and to retrain the operator either directly or through line management. Alternatively, of course, the maintenance engineer could improve the machine so that it can accept rough handling! Training operators in the correct way to handle machines is one of the main jobs of line management and is one which can be strongly supported by maintenance engineers.

Doctor/patient cards for maintenance

We used a simple but easily understood analogy to describe the relationship which we wanted to develop between operators and maintenance personnel: the line operator is the patient and the maintenance engineer is the doctor (Figure 5.1). Doctor/patient cards are used to help support this relationship and to ensure cooperation. On these cards the patient writes down an assessment of the machine condition using these terms:

Figure 5.1   Doctor/patient relationship between maintenance and operators.

Stage 1   Good condition, no problem.
Stage 2   Something wrong.
Stage 3   Problem point, but usable.
Stage 4   Problem point, difficult to use.
Stage 5   Problem point, cannot use.
Stage 6   Broken.

These stages are shown in the 'patient' card in Figure 5.2 as percentages ranging from 100% (no problem) to 0% (broken). The machine described is one of the lug trimmers, which are used for processing the cast lead plates. Machine condition is tracked over consecutive days against eight checking points. The rows headed 'maint' (short for maintenance) allow specific comments to be made.

The 'doctor' card, also shown in Figure 5.2, allows the maintenance engineer to assess how the machine is being operated. Six stages are used, as in the patient card, and the problem points refer to manual operation of the machine. (On the doctor card, there are three columns numbered 1, 2, and 3 for each day because there are three machines of this type in our factory.)

This system is similar to a doctor/patient relationship, where a doctor will be unable to help a patient if the patient does not follow the doctor's orders. The doctor's task is to observe the condition of the patient and ensure that progress towards a healthy condition is being maintained. This simply will not be possible if the patient does not inform the doctor about his or her condition. It is the same thing in the factory. The line operator, as patient, must be alert for abnormal noise or smell, and report the problem point to the maintenance engineer. Such action may well help to prevent a far more serious problem with the machine.

Quality of work

In our company we defined three levels of quality of work (Figure 5.3):

● Repair level work quality;
● Prevention level work quality;
● Improvement level work quality.

Recognition of these three levels of quality of work originated from thinking in our maintenance areas.

Our three-shift production operation threw up many problems. One classic was that of the stainless steel case of a jig which was constantly being damaged because of loose or missing screws. Each time it was damaged, the jig was passed to maintenance. It really was silly for maintenance people to wait until the screws loosened and fell out in this way. But the problems that the jig exposed helped me to explain the three levels of quality of work.

| 100% NO PROBLEM / 80% SOMETHING WRONG / 60% WRONG - CAN BE USED / 40% WRONG - DIFFICULT TO USE / 20% WRONG - CANNOT USE / 0% BROKEN } GIVE NOTICE TO SUPERVISOR | **PATIENT CARD** — LUG TRIMMER No. 1 | Date 6-10-89 Shift A / Checkers Name A. DAVIES / Signature a.Davies |

No.	CHECKING POINT	DATE	6-10-89	7-10-89	8-10-89	9-10-89	10-10-89
1	BLADES NOT RUBBING ON CLAMP	% / MAINT	100	100	100	100	100
2	BLADES NOT MISSING SIDE OF LUG	% / MAINT	100	100	100	100	100
3	NO LOOSE OR BENT CLAMP BARS	% / MAINT	100	100	100	100	100
4	CLAMP HANDLE & PIN SECURE	% / MAINT	100	100	100	100	100
5	TOP PLATE SCREWS SECURE	% / MAINT	100	100	100	80	100
6	BELT NOT SLIPPING OR DAMAGED	% / MAINT	100	100	100	100	100
7	MICRO-SWITCH CORRECT WORKING	% / MAINT	100	100	80	100	100
8	BLADES SHARP	% / MAINT	60	80	60	100	80

| 100% NO PROBLEM / 80% SOMETHING WRONG / 60% WRONG - CAN BE USED / 40% WRONG - DIFFICULT TO USE / 20% WRONG - CANNOT USE / 0% BROKEN } GIVE NOTICE TO SUPERVISOR | **DOCTOR CARD** — LUG TRIMMER | Date 6-10-89 Shift A / Checkers Name J. JONES / Signature J.Jones |

No.	CHECKING POINT	% / MAINT	6-10-89			7-10-89			8-10-89			9-10-89			10-10-89		
			1	2	3	1	2	3	1	2	3	1	2	3	1	2	3
1	BLADE HEIGHT SET BY GAUGE	% / MAINT	100	100	100	100	100	100	100	100	100	100	100	100	100	100	100
2	SHAVING ACTION SLOW & GENTLE	% / MAINT	100	100	60	100	100	100	100	100	100	100	100	100	100	100	100
3	REMOVE LEAD FROM BLADES	% / MAINT	100	60	100	100	100	100	100	100	100	100	100	100	100	100	100
4	CLEAN UNDERNEATH CLAMPS	% / MAINT	80	20	100	100	80	100	100	100	60	100	100	80	80	100	60
5	LUBRICATE CLAMP SLIDES	% / MAINT	60	80	100	100	80	100	100	60	100	100	100	80	80	100	100
6	LUBRICATE CLAMP HANDLE & PIN	% / MAINT	100	60	100	60	80	80	60	100	100	80	100	100	100	60	100
7	WIPE MAIN SLIDE SHAFT	% / MAINT	40	100	100	100	100	100	100	100	60	60	80	100	60	60	80
8	TIGHTNESS OF CLAMPING ASSEMBLY	% / MAINT	100	100	100	100	100	100	100	100	100	100	100	100	100	100	100

Figure 5.2   Examples of doctor and patient cards for maintenance

Level 1: repair

Operators use the jig every day, but after five days the screws fall out and the jig is passed to maintenance so that it can be repaired. Here the maintenance is at a 'repair level', because maintenance is waiting for

Figure 5.3   Three levels of quality of work

the broken tool every day. I defined people who cannot foresee the future and only do the things asked by others as working at a repair level of quality of work.

Level 2: prevention

People begin to recognize a pattern to the intervals in which the screws become loose, and tighten them every four days before they fall off. My definition of this level of quality of work is 'prevention level', where the operator has the ability to foresee the future and to prevent breakdowns.

Level 3: improvement

It is not so clever for the maintenance engineer to tighten the screws every few days. Something is wrong with the design of the screw or the clamping system and the maintenance engineer's task is to redesign the jig so that there is no possibility of screws becoming loose in it. Such a maintenance engineer is at the highest level of quality of work, the improvement level.

These three levels of maintenance activity are illustrated in Figure 4.2. While the levels have been explained here by reference to maintenance, the three levels can be applied to any organization and to any job – to shop floor operators, staff people, engineers, managers and even to managing directors.

Improvement level operators can carefully observe the machines in front of them and identify symptoms of future problems by noticing unusual sounds, distortion or even smells, and prevent a serious problem by making the necessary adjustments to the machine. Later the improvement level operators will propose ideas to eliminate the problem point so that the problems never recur.

A prevention level member of staff can foresee the future, foresee the way the senior person will act, foresee another department's requirement, or the future requirements of the market, and react in advance.

On the other hand, the repair level MD cannot foresee the future of his or her business and simply reacts every day to customer orders or to problems which have arisen in the market or in the company. Such an MD is unable to make a policy for the future for improving the quality of people, environment or product and cannot launch a new product which will fit into future market requirements. A repair level person is 'asked' to do something and simply 'does it'.

Any company has such different levels of people and the challenge for an excellent company is to create many high-level people by training. In a bad company there are many 'repair level' people and some of those cannot even repair correctly: in the worst case they damage the machine or worsen relationships within the organization.

Management (staff) involvement

From an early stage of our project I tried to ensure that all staff people became involved in shop floor problems. We instituted a system of calling staff people to a shop floor problem point; stages depended on the seriousness of the problem, as follows:

Stage 1   Announcement by a line supervisor through the factory speaker system required the maintenance engineer and the technical engineer to run to the line.

Stage 2   Announcement meant that the technical and maintenance supervisors would run to the problem point.

Stage 3   Announcement required all managers and the MD to run to the problem point so that the problem could be dealt with (Figure 5.4).

Figure 5.4   Emergency! It's stage 3. . .

The MD's job in stage 3 is mainly to check whether the organization is working efficiently. The three-stage system ensured that line supervisors could rely on an emergency help system if necessary.

Good cycle or vicious cycle

There is a fundamental difference between the company which is enjoying a good cycle and another company which is on a vicious cycle. Over time the difference becomes very marked and the company on the vicious cycle becomes uncompetitive. It is very easy for a company or department to become trapped in a vicious cycle where, in spite of good intentions, performance spirals downwards.

Again, we can explain this simply in relation to maintenance activities. If a machine breaks down and it takes a long time to repair, many engineers may be tied up in sorting out this one machine. Meanwhile maintenance on other machines is being neglected and so they end up requiring more and more repair work, thus putting further pressures onto the time of the maintenance engineers. This is a typical vicious cycle (Figure 5.5).

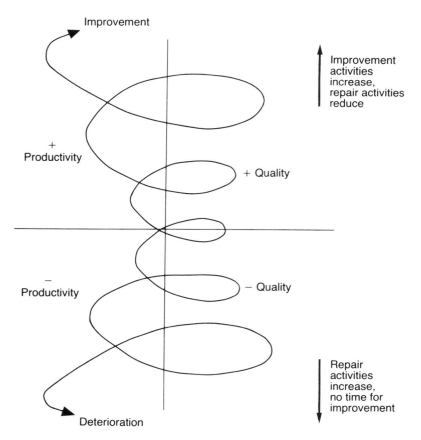

Figure 5.5 Good cycle/vicious cycle

On the other hand the vicious cycle can be broken by predicting which machine is liable to break down and repairing it in advance through a system of preventive maintenance and operator reporting. Once such a system is operating correctly, preventive maintenance takes a shorter time than breakdown maintenance. As a result, maintenance personnel will be able to spend more time checking other machines and also improving them. Once the machines have been improved, maintenance engineers will have even more time to spend on improvement activities. This is a good cycle.

A similar situation can be found in product quality. A complaint about product quality from a customer results in much time and effort being spent in visits, rectification and explaining improvements. During such a visit, the engineer cannot be engaged in improvement activities and so problems continue to multiply.

So if you find a vicious cycle in your factory you must have a very strong intention to get out of the situation, even if it is very hard work to do so and time is short. A key task of top management is to observe the situation in each part of the organization and, if a vicious cycle is found, they must join the struggle with those who are in trouble.

Do automatic machines mean efficiency?

If you have enough money you can buy the most advanced machine available to carry out the manufacturing processes in your company. Companies in Africa, America, India, China, Japan and Britain could all buy the same machine but the efficiency of that machine's utilization depends fairly and squarely on the quality of the people who are going to operate it in the individual company. You cannot buy the people who are going to operate the machine in the same way that you can buy the machine itself. The best operators will come from excellent companies who have developed their people to be disciplined improvers and innovators. If people are not well disciplined, not sensitive enough to find the key problem points, then there will be big differences in machine efficiency as compared with companies who have the best operators.

You can visualize the problem with a ten-station machine consisting of ten robots. If one of the robots develops faults five times a day, there will be 50 stoppages altogether. If it takes two minutes to repair the robot, then 100 minutes of processing time will be lost, which would be a significant problem for expensive equipment. So, unless people are well disciplined and develop good sensitivity for finding and improving problem areas, cheaper labour will actually cost more than highly paid people.

It is essential that industry trains people to have good sensitivity and the ability to take the initiative to sort out problems. It is not easy, but developing excellent people is the biggest investment and asset for the excellent company. The future of the company depends directly on the attitude of its people towards the future.

6 MANAGEMENT AND MANAGEMENT STYLE

In the UK, the word 'fair' is well accepted by everybody. There is a famous saying, 'It isn't cricket', which reflects the fact that people are well trained in fairness through the medium of sport. Fairness in the way that management handles human relations in business is fundamental to success. The meaning of the word 'fair' implies that rules should be kept and applied, and that people never feel that rules seem to apply to them but not to others.

On the golf course, people stop walking if they see that another player is about to make a stroke; they will help to look for their opponent's lost ball and repair pitch marks on the green. I found it impossible to understand why some of the same people throw rubbish onto the pavement in the street, throw away rubbish onto the factory floor, fail to arrive at work on time and break their promises to improve. It is very clear that they have the ability to observe rules and to react fairly, but they are not well trained in the community and in industry. So it must be a problem with society and with the community. However, in industry it is a matter of vital importance and must be addressed.

Fairness in management

To promote the establishment of fairness at work, I established a fundamental philosophy by saying: 'It is unfair if you do not keep to the rules', and illustrated this with the following example. Suppose a person leaves the production line one minute early and the others continue to work. If the manager did not advise that person that he or she must not leave early and a few days passed by, then the other workers would think: 'Why can that person leave early and yet get paid the same wages as us? It is unfair.' As another example, you could point out the person who throws rubbish onto the shop floor, even though they know somebody else will have to go and pick it up. Yet another example would be somebody who is making good-quality batteries which can be sold for money and others who are simply costing us money by making scrap. It is very important for managers to create pressure for fairness to become part of the company culture, and that everyone is encouraged to behave in a fair and correct manner to each other.

Rules and unfairness

Keeping to the rules in a manufacturing business is of vital importance. If operators ignore procedures, the quality of the product will change from day to day. Where products are made in stages which involve many manual processes, you can see how difficult it is to maintain the same quality. Three-shift operation makes it even more difficult as a whole to produce consistent quality. Work on the night shift depends very much on the individual operator's sense of keeping to rules and having a sense of fairness.

Management has a critical role to play in keeping to rules in the same way that a referee observes the rules in a rugby match at Cardiff Arms Park. They must themselves have a strong sense of fairness. They must keep to the rules themselves, for example, by keeping time and by picking up rubbish. Furthermore they must never flinch from emphasizing the concept of unfairness on the shop floor if people leave early, throw down rubbish, write on the toilet wall or store work untidily. Failure to do so has a cascading effect. If a supervisor does not challenge an operator who leaves work one minute early and this goes on for a few days, other operators will follow suit and stop work even earlier.

The reason for other operators following the bad example of the person who leaves work early is simple to explain. They are simply saying to themselves, 'Why should we continue to work while somebody else is allowed to stop early?' If the supervisor did not miss these small points and enforced the concept of fairness by insisting that everybody starts and finishes at the same time, then the rules have been established and people will work to them.

People will follow the rules which have been set fairly by management even if those rules are strict, in the same way that players follow a fair but strict referee. This is a critical point for management to understand. Many managers fail by granting a favour to a group of people without realizing that others will be entitled to ask for the same favour the next day. When the concept of fairness is not applied consistently to everybody, management will collapse.

Discipline: the critical essence of a manufacturing company

If you can maintain discipline, you can maintain consistent quality levels. If you cannot maintain discipline, then you cannot maintain a manufacturing business in the long term. The key point about discipline is that people follow the rules. Applying this to the shop floor, operators must follow manufacturing standards and set procedures every day, every time. In this way, it is possible to maintain quality standards consistently. Many people are apt to think that, if they are required to follow rules strictly, their freedom will simply be reduced. Even worse, it may be felt that the atmosphere for supporting creative work may have been restricted. While it is true that individual freedoms are limited by the need to have common rules for everybody, it is not true that creativity has been reduced at the same time. On the contrary, it is possible for creativity to be made part of the culture by formalizing problem-solving processes and by making them part of everybody's work. It is the same with sport. If rules are interpreted strictly, then the top players will respond by developing their tactics more and more creatively. The referees for the Five Nations rugby matches are very strict, so teams compete by using more creative tactics, decisions and skills.

In business, once rules have been established, people must follow them. But if one of the rules, for example a process procedure, has been found to be lacking, people must make clear the key point of the problem and improve the rule by following certain procedures. Management and staff must always be prepared to improve manufacturing and process standards if a problem point becomes clear. They should not accept complaints and not allow people to blame bad rules for bad results. The principle here is that you should only accept clear problem points for improvement, never complaints.

It is very important that people should follow rules, unless a problem point has been proved and the procedures have been officially changed.

Severity and kindness in management

It is very important for a senior person to use severity in management when it is necessary. The head of any organization has a responsibility to improve that organization to make his people happy in the long term.

The greater the number of people who report to a manager, the greater the responsibility the manager has to subordinates for setting and maintaining standards. If senior people become complacent and allow standards to slip, everybody else will tend to become complacent and the organization will lose its exciting energy and drive. A manager must never shirk the need to be severe for the sake of peace, or eventually respect for the rules of the organization will be lost. So a manager must refuse all temptations to become complacent, and should continually strive to improve a subordinate's performance by increasing the subordinate's targets towards the achievement of a higher level of performance. This may be considered very severe by the subordinate, but it is very important for people to improve themselves and so to allow the company to grow quickly.

The speed at which we can bridge the gap between the ideal position and the present situation depends on the strength of the driving force for improvement. But if a senior person is always managing people severely by raising targets to an unachievable level, a subordinate will lose respect for the manager concerned and hesitate to follow. Therefore the senior person concerned must always show a good example by using his or her own ability to produce ideas and to help subordinates to sort out their problems. In time, the subordinates will recognize their own growth and come to appreciate the manager by realizing that severity is kindness.

Management analogy to sport

Often I found that it was very helpful to use the analogy of sport to explain what I wanted to do in managing the company, and I have used numerous sporting analogies in this book. Because many of our employees typically have a great interest in sport, this analogy can be a very powerful means of getting the message across. The game of rugby has numerous possibilities in itself. For example:

- All players share a love for the game and commitment to their team.
- A player who gets the ball feels a great sense of responsibility for leading the advancement of the team's position in the match.
- Given the limitation of the rules, creativity must be used to develop winning tactics.
- Given the limitation of the rules, you must aim always to develop your own individual skills.
- When you are under pressure during the match, it can be very hard both physically and mentally. But this is still essential to the enjoyment of the sport and the players look back on the tough

moments either with a great sense of achievement or as lessons to be learnt.

- In spite of the fact that individual players have individual personalities, it is only through teamwork that the match can be won.

So there are many similarities between sport and the ideal conditions that management would like to achieve (Figure 6.1). Because local people had such a deep knowledge and understanding of sport, this is something we could build on when they entered the factory gates at Yuasa. The Challange was to develop the same love for work as they would have for rugby as players in Cardiff Arms Park, and to show a similar leadership in creative activities. This could well be the ideal condition for the company. Equally, it would be ideal if company members felt the same sense of relaxation of feeling on leaving the company gates that they do when leaving Cardiff Arms Park.

Figure 6.1   *Another analogy to rugby which we used in our advertisements to emphasize teamwork*

The job of top management is to create the same atmosphere in the company and, even when hard at work, company members should feel a similar sense of satisfaction to that they would experience in sport.

Cleaning the operators' locker room

As we have already discussed, breaking the bad habit of 'them and us' is not easy, but it is crucial to improving the output of individual company members. It is not enough for everybody to wear the same uniform and to use the same canteen, although we have always used both of these practices at Yuasa.

It is very important that all company members demonstrate that they are willing to perform any task that is necessary, including basic duties such as helping out on the shop floor, photo-copying, cleaning and reception duties. In this way all company members can understand each other's job and, more importantly, they can communicate with each other and as a result respect each other more.

Over a period of six years, all managers, including accounting and personnel people, cleaned the operators' locker rooms on the shop floor every day. The key points are to carry out the task every day (as long as I am in the company at the time) and to carry out the work at exactly the same time.

Cleaning the locker room only takes about five minutes and although it is a simple task, sometimes it is the simple tasks which are the most difficult to do. Very often people who cannot do the simple things also do not want to do the difficult things, making excuses all the time. Keeping standards in manufacturing industry is a most important matter, and standards should be a combination of simple things. A manual of manufacturing standards means nothing if people ignore it. They must have a discipline in advance to observe rules, even if the rules relate to small things. In manufacturing, doing the simple things correctly is the vital habit of ensuring quality.

Cleaning the locker room arose from a direct experience which I had. When we started our production operations, the inside of the factory became very dirty and I could see rubbish everywhere. I asked the factory manager to get our company members to keep the factory clean. But the situation did not improve at all. At first I thought that this was because there was not enough cleaning equipment installed at convenient places, so I advised the supervisors to place cleaning materials at suitable points around the factory. They replied that the idea was very risky because somebody woud steal them unless we kept them in a lockable steel cabinet. But I argued that, if the tools were locked away in a steel cabinet, it would be very difficult for anybody to be able to use them. So I insisted that they should be installed in positions where everybody could see them and they would be easy to use. I argued that, if the company trusted its members and kept all areas of the factory clean, it would actually be very difficult for somebody to steal the tools. So we went ahead and installed the tools, but several weeks afterwards nobody had started to use them because they did not think that cleaning the factory was part of their job. If managers and supervisors tried to start cleaning, they would lose respect because people thought that cleaning was a cleaner's job. That was why I decided to do the job myself with other managers. I have continued to carry out this task for over six years with other voluntary staff people, such as senior supervisors and managers (Figure 6.2).

Figure 6.2   Cleaning the locker room five minutes every day

To begin with, shop floor reaction was not good. The feeling was that staff people should do their own job. But gradually, as time passed, people came to understand the purpose of our actions and this has helped to break the 'them and us' attitude which existed between staff and shop floor. Seeing managers regularly perform these tasks helped to dispel the thought that the tasks were too menial for the operator and helped to encourage company members to accept other duties that were needed outside their daily operating routines. So people have behaved in a flexible way almost unconsciously.

Cleaning the shop floor locker room every day at exactly the same time highlighted fundamental management points:

● *Time consciousness*   Good time keeping is the most fundamental point of discipline. In a three-shift operation, time keeping is not so easy and supervisors sometimes extend their meetings unconsciously and fail to keep their promises, with many excuses. Staff people often do the same. So that a good example could be shown in time consciousness by managers, staff and shop floor people, cleaning every day at exactly the same time was both good training and a good demonstration. In order to be on the shop floor on time, staff people had to finish meetings five minutes before ten o'clock, and in order to achieve this they always had to be conscious of time.

● *No excuses*   In the beginning many staff people could not attend the cleaning sessions at ten o'clock and came up with numerous excuses, but whatever happened I always kept time and set a good example by always arriving at ten o'clock. Gradually people hesitated to arrive late with excuses and became more conscious of time. It also meant that people tried to carry out their meetings more efficiently and to make out a schedule to cover every hour of every day. In other words people gradually came to understand the meaning of the old proverb, 'Where there's a will, there's a way.'

We also insisted that company members should keep their locker rooms tidy and that uniforms should be hung in the places provided. A dim view was taken of anybody who simply threw their uniform on the floor. The first objection to such actions was obviously on health and safety grounds but just as important was the necessity to be able to keep basic routines and disciplines. If an operator cannot perform very simple tasks, even that of hanging up uniforms correctly, then it is difficult to insist that more difficult production processes are followed consistently.

The challenge of QE III

There are many disadvantages for a newly-established company, not least of which is recruiting people with appropriate skills. Typically the skills and experience required will be non-existent or difficult to recruit because the company has an unknown track record. However there is the clear advantage that recruits will not have preconceived ideas and can be moulded into the new company culture more easily. In our case, the disadvantages of very distant technical support from Japan was offset by the reduced influence of Japanese culture. This meant that we could create our own culture which best suited our own local conditions. One method used to generate this good 'spiritual' environment was the concept of the QE III.

The QE III was always used to portray our future company situation; that is, that we would be the number one company in the world in our business by 1988. In our early years, during salary review or on other relevant occasions, company performance was described as a vessel at sea, gradually increasing in size and performance, from a rowing boat through tugs and liners until we reached the final goal – the biggest liner in the world, QE III (Figure 6.3). Mottoes such as those listed in Chapter 4 were used to urge us on our way. We feel that the team spirit which they engendered was essential in helping us to attain the Queen's Award for Export after only three years in production. The award also helped us on our way in our drive to become the number one battery manufacturer and was an achievement in which all company members could take pride.

Figure 6.3   The Challenge of QE III . . . aiming for world No. 1

Just-in-Time

Just-in-Time in a factory is an excellent system from the following points of view.

- A problem can be raised clearly and immediately.
- A problem automatically affects all processes in the factory, so everybody gets to know about it.

As a result of the second point, every problem becomes a major problem and so becomes everybody's concern.

You cannot buy a Just-in-Time system in the same way that you can buy a machine, with money. Attaining a Just-in-Time production system means that you must have achieved a certain level in the quality of people, for the following reasons:

- The person at each process must feel responsible for problems and always try to avoid them. If an operator simply blames a machine breakdown on someone else, a Just-in-Time system will not work. People must accept ownership of the problem.
- Operators must be capable of maintenance work and have the sensitivity to spot symptoms in advance of serious damage to a machine. They should be trained in and capable of preventive maintenance.
- When other processes stop and people cannot do their work because components are not available, they must have the drive to immediately start QC circle or preventive maintenance activities.

Thus achieving Just-in-Time in your own manufacturing processes is very difficult and a lot of company-wide effort is required.

On the other hand, if a company is doing Just-in-Time successfully, it is clear evidence of an excellent company in which line operators are carrying out both excellent preventive maintenance work and creative activities to prevent problems in their own processes.

It is very difficult to introduce Just-in-Time quickly. In our company I introduced Just-in-Time in three stages:

- *First Stage* Developing interest among shop floor people in QC circle activities. Achieving a systematic approach to problem solving.
- *Second Stage* Promoting line operators' responsibility for their machines. Introduction of doctor/patients cards for maintenance. Awareness of three levels of maintenance, and development of expertise in preventive maintenance.
- *Third Stage* Introduction of simple kanban* system which is easy to use.

In order to support the introduction of the third stage, we developed a simple kanban rack. The storage rack in each process has a big hanging label attached to it, indicating the charge of the product in process (positive or negative). Labels are coloured yellow and red, and the rule is that you must continue to produce to fill empty places in the rack (Figure 6.4). Red label instructions must be completed first and if all red racks are full then you can follow the yellow instructions. Once both yellow and red are full, you should stop production and do maintenance or QC activities instead. The merit of this system is that everybody knows what the production requirements are without production control giving out daily instructions.

*For a definition of kanban see the glossary on p83.

Suppliers

Products are the integration of many components. A company cannot properly achieve such integration by itself. It is well known that the strength of Japanese car companies results from the integration of the strength of their suppliers. It took a long time for Japanese car companies to achieve good-quality, reliable suppliers. Now they know each other, they communicate well and they know what they should do. 'Levelling up' suppliers carries almost the same importance as any manufacturer levelling up itself. While a low price for a component is important, the ability of the supplier to produce a component at low cost is more important.

In the UK, my process for selecting a supplier company was as follows:

1   Study the quality of the product, including its variability.
2   Study the price and volume, and compare with others.
3   Study the experience and history of the company.
4   Visit the company.

- Study the brightness of the company member's eye.
- Study people's movement and tidiness.
- Study the factory tidiness and efficiency of material movements.
- Study the MD's policy and character.
- Discuss the supply with the relevant managers, and judge the ability of each.

If the company is small, then the most important thing is the MD's policy and character. If his or her policy is clear and there is evidence of striving to improve things, then you can confirm the evidence of this attitude in the factory and in discussion with company members. If both are good, then things look very promising so far.

5   Gauge whether the price is reasonable. Sometimes suppliers try to quote a lower price in order to get the business and have a problem later on.

Once we have selected the supplier, we communicate well and try to make the supplier into an excellent company as well as ourselves. It is most important for manufacturers and suppliers to understand each other, to exchange ideas often and to strive to increase efficiency and maintain competitiveness in that industry. A relationship based on price alone will be far less effective than one based on partnership. Any company can survive and will thrive in an industry if it can be the most efficient company in that industry. In general it has been the Japanese custom in Japan for a manufacturer to ask suppliers to lower their prices every year by implementing ideas for cost reduction.

On the other hand, it has been the recognized Western custom for suppliers to ask manufacturers for a higher price every year as a result of inflation in wages, material prices, greater investment and so on. Over a period of a few years, this results in tremendous price differences between Japanese and Western suppliers.

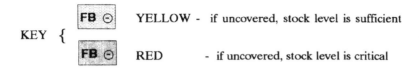

KEY {

FB ⊖ YELLOW - if uncovered, stock level is sufficient

FB ⊖ RED - if uncovered, stock level is critical

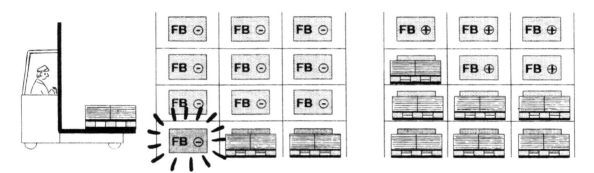

Figure 6.4 Kanban racking system for storing charged plates between plate preparation and final assembly

7 ON REFLECTION

Britain and Japan are both island nations located next to continental land masses. The latitude of Britain is far higher than that of Japan (the northernmost part of Japan, Hokkaido, is in the same latitude as Spain). Britain has a warm winter and a comfortable summer as a result of the Gulf Stream, while Japan has snowy winters and hot, very humid summers. I came to love the British climate because it is comparatively mild and gentle throughout the year. Although there are many wet days, rainfall is not so great compared with Japan. There are always beautiful clouds to admire, and the British cannot complain too much about the wet days needed to maintain the beautiful green land!

The place where I lived in Wales is an especially lovely spot: I really believe that it is the most lovely place in the world. The mountains, rivers, lakes and moorlands create pleasant, spacious views on all sides. I used to enjoy the beautiful sunset from the moor on the way back home. Beautiful clouds changed colour from grey to pink to gold and died out in the dusk. We can enjoy the sunset much longer in Britain than in Japan because of the high latitude. With such spacious views, people enjoy being outside. On holiday, or in the summer evenings, some just stop their car beside the road and sit there admiring the scenery. Others enjoy boating in the canals, while young people can enjoy outdoor sports like caving, rock climbing and sailing, as well as rugby and car racing. There are so many things to do!

British youngsters grow up to enjoy these things, but in Japan there are not so many opportunities for people to experience the pleasures of outdoor life. Although there is a trend for young people to enjoy some sports, these are less popular than in the UK because the price of land in Japan limits opportunities.

Older Japanese people who experienced the war have simply tried to survive and bring up their families. They have attached great importance to the education of their children. Such pressures have led to the notorious 'examination hell' for the children, who are forced to compete from a very early age. In this sense, Japanese people become accustomed to pressure. The combination of the seniority system, lifetime employment (which helps teamwork) and the habit of being pressured has helped Japanese industry to overcome many difficult times, such as the opening up of world markets, and the oil shocks. Japanese industries have utilized these pressures as opportunities to improve themselves. On the other hand, Britain has not had such strong pressures, and so was not in a good position to utilize those pressures as opportunities for improvement.

I think that the future will be different. In recent years Japan has had a relatively comfortable time, with low inflation, low unemployment, low oil prices and an expanding domestic market. Such comfortable conditions will tend to weaken the strength of Japanese industry. Japanese young people are changing too – they have learned to enjoy themselves better. They like more holidays and less work. As unemployment continues to fall, they feel they can easily find a job. If they do not like it, they can change their job easily, which means that the seniority system is gradually collapsing. On the other hand, European people are getting excited about the prospects of 1992 and beyond. People's views of industry are changing as a result of changing government attitudes towards industry.

In the future, management style will change both in Britain and in Japan. Management in Japan will no longer be able to ask people to work hard out of a sense of duty. Without stimulating an individual interest in the job it will no longer be possible to get the best efficiency in the team. I have tried to introduce a new management style which promotes an individual's interest in work. I set about this by using the similarity between enjoyment in sport and enjoyment in business, stressing the need for the individual to improve themselves in both company and society, and by creating an atmosphere of freedom for the individual to think for themselves. Initially the last point embarrassed people who were working by simply following the instruction of the senior person. The reason we created these approaches is based on the different environment of people's attitudes in Britain. But recent trends in Japan are towards a similar environment. In this sense I hope that my ideas will have an impact on industry in both countries for the future.

Good people, good company

In the long run, 'good company' simply means a company which has good people of high potential. When you visit an excellent manufacturing company on a Sunday, you can see only excellent machines there. Maybe there is even a computer-integrated manufacturing system. But without people it will not work, and it is not always true that, when the people return to work on Monday, the company works well. Although proper investment is always important, true competition is not in buying sophisticated machines, but in operating these sophisticated machines efficiently. Sophisticated machines need good operators. Bad operators greatly reduce the value of the investment to the company. Fundamentally the operator's job is the same whether the machine is sophisticated or simple. There is always the need to detect deviations from standard through observation, immediate analysis and corrective action, as well as following standard routine operations. If operators ignore operating standards they will cause problems. If operators do not have the ability to observe, they will miss the problems. These fundamental abilities cannot be achieved by training straightaway. They can only be achieved through lengthy on-the-job training so that they become habits.

The same fundamental points apply to work in the office. Routine work should be done correctly, but in the future it will be carried out by computer. When your routine work is computerized, your work will be reduced by that amount. On the other hand, the ability to observe and to identify problems is more important at any time. You can continue to enjoy your work even after part of it has been computerized because you have more time to find problems, to sort them out and to improve your work. Therefore your work will be more creative and human.

One supervisor cannot train all operators and one manager cannot train all supervisors. Developing good habits can only be achieved by everybody's effort and understanding, and by the long-term, continuous energy of the management.

My definition of good people is well-disciplined, creative people. Well-disciplined people respect the rules and standards, and they can communicate correctly with the whole organization. Creativity requires observation, analysis, spotting the key point, producing ideas and implementing them to improve the task. People who can do this will work well in any organization and in any position. That means that they can enjoy their work all the time. A company which has succeeded in training people in this way will no doubt be successful in the future. People are the company's most important asset, and that is why I look at the brightness of people's eyes and the tidiness of the factory when I visit a company to study its performance. The brightness of people's eyes is a good indicator of their creativity, and the tidiness of the factory shows the degree of discipline of the people working there. Sometimes these observations are more important than the documented performance of the company.

In this sense I am sure of my belief that 'only good people can make a good company'. The same could be said for the community as a whole. To support good industry, everybody's effort in the community is needed.

The attractiveness of industry

Industry can give people the chance to extend their skills in many areas, such as art, science, music and law. Without such diverse skills, industries cannot perform efficiently or provide an appropriate environment for work, or a focus for the community. Capable entrepreneurs set out to paint on a business canvas with a set philosophy for the art of management. The canvas reflects the leader's sense of balance and layout, and the highlights change every day, yet still preserve a balanced beauty. Similarly, managers should control company members as a conductor controls the orchestra, so that individuals can give their best performance in real harmony.

But if you want to become a good industrialist it is important to have a good scientific mind so that you can solve problems efficiently, according to the methods outlined in Chapter 3. Without this logical approach to solving problems, you cannot react correctly and efficiently to the different problems which change from day to day.

Manufacturing industry is more complex than other professions such as the money market, politics, pure research or human science, in the sense that it requires integration of company members, suppliers and customers. There are so many variables which need to be controlled in order to improve. You cannot manufacture so much as one product item if you break the laws of natural science. Equally you cannot run the business if you ignore human science.

Market research can tell you which product will fit the market, but this is not enough. The product must be attractive enough to be competitive in design, function and cost. Yet it will not be competitive in any of these areas unless it satisfies each customer's needs during its working lifetime. Even then, the product may need to be confirmed as being environmentally safe. Without integrating skills in all of these areas industry will not expand in a healthy condition towards the future.

This is what makes industry more challenging and more attractive to young people, in that they can exercise and develop all of their abilities. While money is a necessary motivator, enjoying every hour of your life through challenge every day is more important to the individual. Young people must learn to understand the business environment while they are at school. They must learn about the attractive and challenging aspects of this environment from their teachers and, to achieve this, first of all let the teachers themselves understand the really attractive, challenging life which industry can provide. Only experienced industrialists truly know about these things. Industry has always been the most important aspect of our history and has supported culture and civilization at each stage of man's development.

Future management

It has been said that Japanese managers are trained as generalists and can carry out a wide range of duties, but that their Western counterparts are trained as specialists. I think that there are advantages and disadvantages in both cases. If the Western way limits the flexibility of work, and as a result limits the range of people's interests, then in this sense it incorporates a disadvantage. In recent rugby strategy, the 'all-round player' system has been employed. A team can attack more efficiently if each of the players possesses a wide range of skills. On the other hand, if the Japanese way limits the individual's deep interest in creativity, this aspect is a disadvantage. The best top managers are those who have experienced work in many divisions because they have developed an improved ability to know how to increase individual output. Company performance is the integration of individual outputs, provided that the direction of the company has been correctly set.

Future management style will be a combination of both Western and Japanese approaches, and will be based more on individual creativity. In the twenty-first century an increasing number of information systems will be developed and information will be open to all company members. Each member of each organization reacts to the same information in different ways to share work needed to reach company objectives without being instructed by senior managers. Instead the manager's job will be the adjustment of company direction, developing a creative environment for the company and correctly evaluating the individual. Future activities for Yuasa Battery (UK) are represented in Figure 7.1.

Links with Total Quality

Total Quality programmes (in many versions such as TQC and TQM) are now popular in Japan and in many countries across the world. The main reason that I have not referred to Total Quality in this book is that I believe that there is something more important that needs to be done before setting out to implement such a system. My reasons for thinking this way are as follows:

- *Discipline*   This is critical to the being of a manufacturing company, as was explained in the last chapter. People must follow the rules. If discipline is not good then data are unreliable and computer figures are meaningless.
- *People motivation*   At work people must be encouraged by the promotion of a good environment for creative activities.

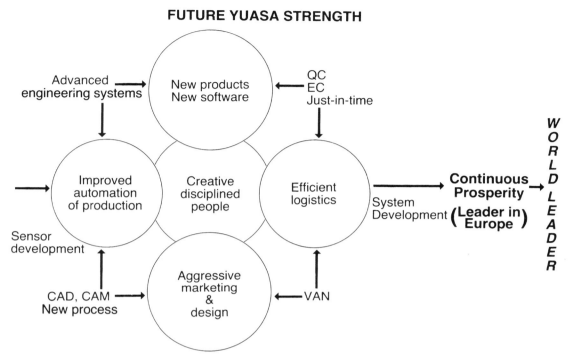

Figure 7.1   Vision of the development of Yuasa

Developing our own business system by ourselves is more enjoyable than applying a well-established system. Further, I was afraid that people would be demotivated if they were asked to apply some established system: it might reduce their own creativity and they might lose the chance of increasing their ability to improve. Once we start to create our own business system by ourselves, we develop our own ability to evaluate other systems and then we can easily employ the good points of other systems (Figure 7.2). In this sense making well-disciplined and creative people should precede the application of important management systems.

The relationship between my views and other systems for business improvement is shown in Figure 7.3.(a), (b) and (c). These represent different versions of the improvement process – individual, business and innovation. The three versions are based on similar grounds. The outer circle is like the well-known 'Plan – Do – Check – Action' (PDCA) or 'Shewhart Cycle' of improvement. But I have emphasized and made more explicit the process of generating ideas.

Working from the outside, the diagrams have four steps, numbered 1 to 4 in Figures 7.3 (a) to (c). Steps 1, 2 and 3 roughly correspond respectively to the Plan–Do–Check steps of the Shewhart

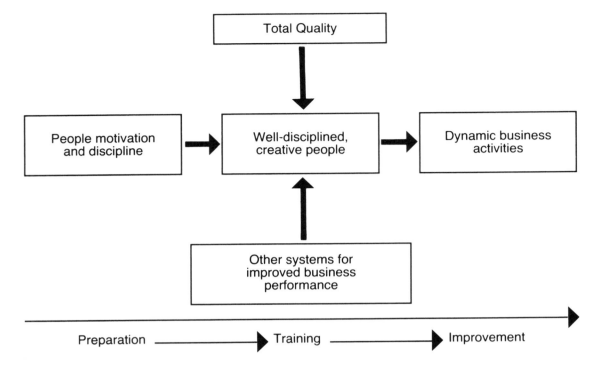

Figure 7.2   People motivation and discipline: the first step towards an excellent company

cycle. I have added a fourth step in the 'creativity' area, which is more important in the Business Action (Figure 7.3b) and Improvement (Figure 7.3c) Cycles. In the Human Social Behaviour Cycle (Figure 7.3a), step 4 can be less creative — sometimes only the selection of a preferred option from a number of alternatives offered. So instead of making ideas, a lady may simply select a dress from those available in her wardrobe, or a person may choose a car from a range offered at a garage. Decisions like these are happening all the time in everyday life: people follow the social behaviour cycle unconsciously. Often the goals themselves are not clear, and the option selected may simply be a choice made on the spur of the moment. People do routine things in life like washing dishes by limiting the creative steps to making judgements only (for example, is this cup clean enough?), and by acting accordingly. The goal is a repetitive one, so it becomes blurred over time and there is no pressure to make ideas. But the key steps are followed. Outside information may show it is a fine day, so we have the idea of going out to the shops. After structuring our idea, we make a plan and then go to the shops. Perhaps the data we observe after shopping indicates we have spent too much, so we amend our ideas for next time!

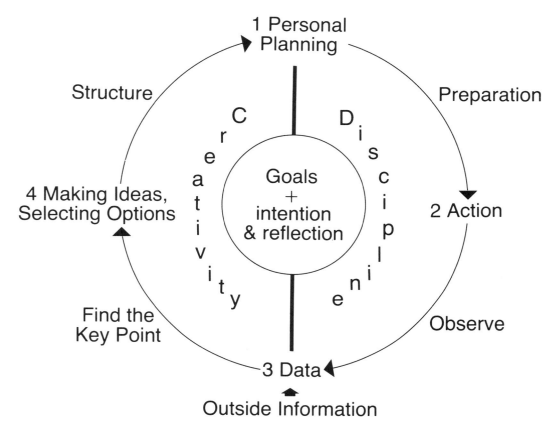

Figure 7.3(a)   Human social behaviour cycle

I have already stressed the importance of the areas within the outer circle by referring to the discipline environment (1,2,3 on the diagrams) and to the creativity (idea-making) environment (3,4,1 on the diagrams). In future, businesses will gradually replace the discipline area (1,2,3) by computers and automation, and the accent will be on the creativity area (3,4,1).

At the core of each cycle are the key elements in promoting the creativity and discipline environments. These key elements are goals, together with the interest or drive to achieve them (intention), and the ability to learn and to apply that learning (reflection). Each cycle revolves around this basic nucleus of human behaviour. Successful TQC can only be achieved by first establishing this nucleus and then by combining it with the activities in the outer circle.

Figure 7.3.(a) illustrates how planning, acting and responding to data relate to the 'discipline' which is exerted by that person to achieve the goals. On the left hand side of the diagram the person's ability to

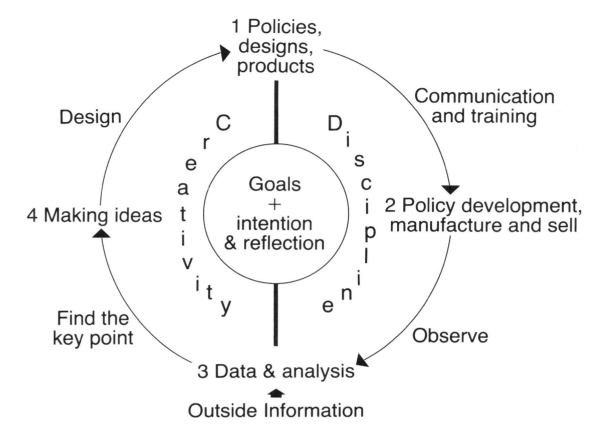

Figure 7.3(b)   Business action cycle

use data to make judgements and decisions and to feed those back into the planning process reflects the ability to use 'creativity' towards achieving goals.

The business action diagram shown in Figure 7.3(b) is very similar: the 'planning' phase of the social behaviour cycle is converted to the business's designs and products; the 'action' phase becomes the manufacture and sale of goods and services. So the relative discipline of the business reflects the ability of the company members accurately to convert such designs into conforming products. The process of making ideas at step 4 is more emphasized in business. Improvement is the key to the company's competitive strength. Company members must follow all steps of the cycle all the time, so the goals must be clear and the communication and training must be good. In this way, the company can get into a good cycle, and fresh ideas help performance to spiral up (see Figure 5.5). If things are not going well, on the other

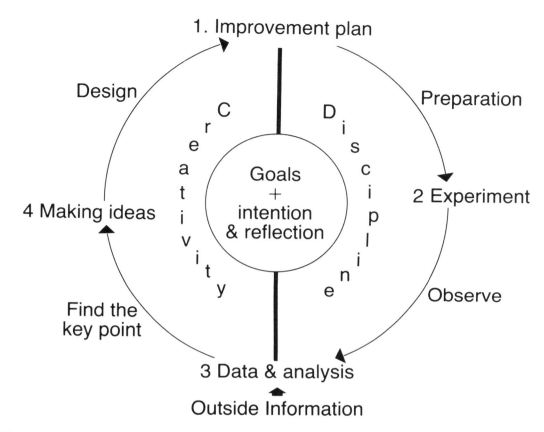

Figure 7.3(c) Improvement cycle

hand, then it is necessary to find in which part of the business action cycle that performance is weak. For example, my concept of a 'repair level' operator is one whose abilities are limited to the right hand portion of this diagram. At work, his or her ability to make judgements and decisions is suppressed for some reason. It is necessary to endeavour to convert such a person into an 'improvement level' operator by opening up their creative abilities. In an excellent company, many people have developed capabilities on both sides of this diagram, while in a bad company most people follow orders or systems like machines.

Likewise, the Managing Director must make plans and policies for the business. All such directions for the business must be co-ordinated by the top team. Sometimes, ideas for policies come from subordinates who have analysed outside information and presented their ideas to the top team as a 'bottom up' set of proposals. On other occasions, the Managing Director may decide on a policy, and it is developed by subordinates at step 2. If the data analysed at step 3 is not good, the Managing Director must reflect and improve the communication, find the key point of what went wrong, and develop new ideas for fresh policies. For the company to become an excellent one, it must be possible to analyse information dynamically, so that new ideas are continuously being generated for policies, designs and products by the creative abilities of the company's members.

The process of innovation itself is illustrated in Figure 7.3 (c). Notice that the process still revolves around set goals underpinned by intention and reflection. The external stages are similar to the problem-solving routine shown in Table 3.1. The ability to apply ideas and to observe results relates to the discipline of the improvement activity. Because of the similarity of the three cycles (social behaviour, business action and improvement) it is possible to lay the three diagrams on top of each other, as in Figure 7.3(d). This shows how the excellent company is centred on goals underpinned by intention and reflection and by well-developed creativity and discipline.

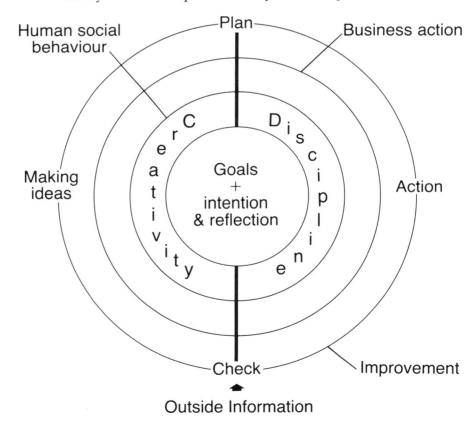

Figure 7.3(d)   *Total human action cycle for excellence*

Conclusion

I set out to create an ideal management approach which would be strong enough to compete with Japanese companies in Japan. The industrial environment needed to be taken into account. It comprised ways of life, the nature of people and customs for conducting business (including suppliers and customers). In the different Western environment, I could not introduce the Japanese way directly. The route that I chose was to set out to transform the essence of the successful Japanese way into a new way which would be successful in a Western environment. The relationship between the Japanese way and my model for the transformed way is shown in Table 7.1.

Firstly, I listed the good aspects of the Japanese way. Then I developed the essential points of the Japanese way by discarding Japanese specialities such as tradition and habit. Finally I added back Western specialities to the essential points to develop a 'successful Western way'. The diagram works as follows:

1 Traditional conservation of teamwork

Japan has had a long feudal history of rice farming in small fields whereby people who formed the small communities could not survive unless they cooperated as a team. This flexibility and small-group activity was maintained because of the need to start work from scratch after the destruction of the Second World War. Because teamwork activity benefits the industrial environment, I selected this aspect in column 3 as the essential point of the successful Japanese way. However, to realize such a team spirit in the industrial environment at Ebbw Vale, I could not use the tradition which applies in Japan. Therefore I discarded the Japanese speciality and replaced it with the Western speciality of sport and games. Ebbw Vale people enjoy teamwork in sport, and so I tried to introduce a sporting spirit into my management style: for example, the meaning of rules, productivity competitions between shifts and QC circle competitions.

2 Loyalty to work

This successful Japanese way has been fostered by lifetime employment and the seniority system whereby a company member could rely on the company and the company in turn could rely on its members. In a young company situated in a Western industrial environment, I could not ask company members to be loyal to the company. Therefore I discarded the Japanese speciality and substituted the Western speciality of individualism. Working for one's own good is a very strong incentive in the West, and so creates a very good opportunity. If working for oneself means working for money only, then this opportunity will be wasted. However, if management can succeed in developing an exciting work environment, people can enjoy their life through work by having the opportunity to develop and meet their own goals.

Table 7.1   Transformation of the management approach

	Successful Japanese way	Discard Japanese speciality	Essential points	Add Western speciality	Successful Western way
1	Traditional conservation of teamwork	Tradition from feudal past	Teamwork activity	Sport, games	Encourage a sporting spirit in work
2	Loyalty to work	To the company	Loyalty	Individualism	Work for himself/herself
3	QC circle motivation	Group behaviour	Interest	Sport, games	Promote individual interest
4	Working is respectable	Society view	Value of working life	Time consciousness and excitement in life	Being excited about and being conscious of the importance of life at work
5	Work together (management and workforce)	Working from scratch after Second World War	Integrated teamwork	Sport, family activities	Supervisors and managers set good example in working together. Eliminate 'them and us'
6	Flexibility in work	Working from scratch after Second World War	Curiosity	'Do-it-yourself' car maintenance	Promote interest of individual and provide opportunities No demarcation
7	Seniority system	Traditional conservativeness	On the job training and evaluation of experience	Community activity	On the job training and domestic promotion
8	Lifetime employment	Traditional conservativeness	Job change and promotion	Moving jobs and community activities	Domestic job moves and promotion

**3
QC circle
motivation**

As I indicated under 'The Basis for Japanese Success' in Chapter 1, Japanese companies have benefited from group activities, especially after the Second World War. Group activities have been cultivated to overcome the many depressions that have been experienced and which would otherwise destroy the basis for lifetime employment. But the essential point of QC circle activities should be the interest in individual members. Sport and games again provide many people with the opportunity for creating new individual skills. Here the Western speciality can be used to promote the individual interest of team members.

**4
Working is
respectable**

A Japanese industrialist has a higher status in society than does his British counterpart. If people working in industry cannot take pride in their work, this downgrades the individuals and the company concerned. 'The Attraction of Industry' in this chapter refers to the opportunities which industry provides to people for developing their abilities under a very wide range of challenges during that valuable part of their life – their time at work. And enjoying all aspects of your life is a fundamental human right.

**5
Work
together**

Japanese management and workforces were forced to work together starting from scratch after the disasters of the Second World War. But the essential need is for integrated teamwork by all company members. Here the Western specialities of teamwork in sport and family life can be directed at eliminating the 'them and us' residues of class consciousness. Above all, integrated teamwork needs the good example of managers all working together.

**6
Flexibility
in work**

Again, this was promoted by the necessity of starting from scratch after the Second World War, but I took the essential point of flexibility in work to be curiosity. A complementary speciality is interest in the challenge of hobbies such as 'do it yourself' and car maintenance. If companies can provide individual members with the opportunities to develop their own interest and curiosity, no doubt such people will become flexible in work.

**7
Seniority
system**

The essential point here is the recognition of the value of experience. This can be strengthened by natural social behaviour in Western society which values experience. In Japan, people are continuously developed by means of on-the-job training, so that older people normally have wider abilities than younger ones. While an excellent company does not have to embrace the seniority system, on-the-job training must be adopted and so must the evaluation of the progress of trainers and trainees. Furthermore it is essential to give proper opportunities for job rotation and promotion within the company.

**8
Lifetime
employment**

The lifetime employment custom in Japan has already been showing signs of change. The essential point here is the continuous interest in work being encouraged by job change and promotion. People are always changing their jobs in Western companies, but they do seem to enjoy their various community activities. So, if a company can provide the challenge of continuous interest in work by providing opportunities for changing jobs and promotion, then people will stay in that company for a long time, as can be seen in excellent companies around the world.

The Japanese industrial environment has been changing quickly in recent years, growing more like the Western environment. I hope that the essence of our experiment in the UK can be applied in the future to Japanese industry.

Because each country has its own specialities, I hope that the approach summarized in Table 7.1 can be used to develop the essential points of an excellent company by adding on its own specialities in order to achieve excellent industries. For example, the change to a free market economy in many Eastern Bloc countries will not of itself make it so easy to catch up with Western companies. Rather, countries should recognize the strengths within individual cultures and use those strengths to make the essential points work for them. The objective is to make each country and its people wealthy and prosperous. To achieve this, all people must strive to work creatively and with good application.

Key Points

Chapter 1
Setting out to compete with Japan

- A strategy to beat Japanese companies based in Japan:
  - quality levels must be equal or better;
  - productivity levels must be matched;
  - three-shift operation should be established.
- Break the bad habits: how can we develop good working practices in a UK setting?
  - developing the same motivation at work as is shown for sports and hobbies.
- Continuous improvement – the pressure to reduce costs and hold prices.
- The fundamental factors for success:
  - increasing the output of all company members;
  - advancing the company in the correct direction.
- Overcoming the effects of depressions and competitor activity helps a business to grow.
- Setting out to create our own management systems which would be competitive against the Japanese methods:
  - combining good management practices from both Japan and the West;
  - encouraging all company members to find fulfilment at work.

Chapter 2
Personal policies

- Breaking bad habits:
  - a key task, led by management;
  - destroy 'them and us' throughout the company;
  - flexible working practices start with management;

encourage dialogue between functions;
repeatedly communicate what you want.
- Developing good people:
    people are an asset whose value increases each year;
    the objective: well disciplined, creative people;
    promote from within to reward improvement;
    take great care in selection;
    on-the-job training.
- Rewarding ability:
    improve ability first and the money will follow;
    continuously monitor your subordinates' ability.

Chapter 3
Improvement

- Improvement is a creative activity which results from the intention to achieve better things.
- Generating an interest in work is a key point for success:
    interest stimulates the creativity to do things better.
- QC circles: a mechanism to attack problems systematically and collectively:
    train circle members;
    recognize efforts;
    use every opportunity for presentations;
    develop the sensitivity of company members.
- Excuses are a waste of time:
    do not allow people to make them;
    find the key point.
- Improvement activities distinguish the excellent company:
    routine tasks become mechanized;
    only improvement remains.

Chapter 4
Communication

- Company information is there to be shared:
    but different levels in the company react to it in different ways.
- Complaints (like excuses) achieve nothing:
    identify the key point;
    implement overlapping responsibilities between line and staff etc.
- Multi-purpose plant tours:
    shorten lines of communication;

break down barriers;
show senior managers are there to help.
● Communication must be promoted by carefully designed initiatives appropriate to the company:
multi-communication meetings promote flexibility between members of staff;
morning speeches help people understand my philosophy;
advisory board promotes involvement of company and trade union representatives;
'open plan' general office;
visual display.

Chapter 5
Maintenance

● Break down barriers:
do not accept complaints;
foster cooperation in solving problems between line and staff;
use doctor/patient cards to identify the relative seriousness of problems.
● Quality of work:
repair level: cannot foresee the future;
prevention level: can foresee the future;
improvement level: can influence the future.
*A key management task is to convert more and more people into the improvement level.
● Look out for vicious cycles:
they mean more time spent on repair level activities and less on improvement activities.
● The efficiency of machines is a direct reflection on the quality of people who operate them.

Chapter 6
Management and management style

● It is unfair not to observe the rules:
it is a management task to create pressure for upholding fairness at work;
keeping to the rules in a manufacturing business is vital.
● Discipline: the critical essence of a manufacturing company:
the need to do it the same way every time;

apply the rules strictly;
if a rule is lacking, do not complain about it: identify the problem point and get it changed;
manufacturing standards mean nothing if people ignore them;
do the simple things right;
severeness is kindness.

- Cleaning the operators' locker room: a lesson in management flexibility.
- Maintaining the vision of an ideal company: the 'challenge of QE III'.
- Just-in-Time should be introduced in stages as the company improves.
- The need to 'level up' suppliers as well as our own company.

Chapter 7
On reflection

- Good people, good company
  good people are well disciplined and creative.
- Automation means removing routine, disciplined work and leaving more time for creative activities.
- Before embarking on Total Quality, develop the business by ensuring:
  discipline to follow the rules;
  foster an environment which motivates people to take part in creative activities.
- The route to improvement:
  clear goals, underpinned by strong intention and reflection;
  discipline when making actions, manufacturing products etc;
  creativity in developing new ideas, designing new products or systems, etc.
- Transform Japanese successful ways into successful ways appropriate to western culture:
  team work
  loyalty
  interest
  value in working life
  integration
  curiosity
  value of experience
  job rotation and promotion

Glossary of Terms

Buffer stocks   A company may be able to forecast an average demand for its products, and aim to keep stocks of products in line with that forecast. But what if actual demand is different from the forecast? The company will keep in addition a buffer stock (or safety stock) to protect its level of customer service from inaccurate forecasts of demand. Buffer stocks of raw materials and work in progress may be held in the same way as buffer stocks of finished products.

CAD   CAD stands for computer aided design, and refers to the application of computers in design and analysis. It aims to increase design productivity, reduce design lead times, provide three-dimensional simulations, etc.

CAM   CAM stands for computer aided manufacturing, and refers to the use of computers and micro-processors to manufacturing processes. CAM typically refers to the use of computers to speed up the setting and operation of numerically controlled (NC) machine tools, but is also used to refer to the wider application of computers in manufacturing — for example, in production control.

EC   EC stands for engineering circles, and describes the use of joint problem-solving teams to study engineering problems and to propose solutions (*cf* Quality Control Circles below).

Fish-bone charts   This approach to problem solving was developed by the famous Japanese 'guru' Kaoru Ishikawa. An example is shown in Figure G.1. Here the problem (damaged batteries at terminal weld) was analysed under three main causes (manual, machine and materials). The QC circle brain-storms ideas as sub causes and sub-sub causes, so that all possible factors are considered. The chart may end up looking like a series of fish-bones — hence its name! The circle then votes on the most important factor, and repeats the process until the key points have been identified.

Just-in-Time (JIT)   Just-in-Time is the western embodiment of a philosophy and supporting production techniques developed and perfected by the Japanese. The philosophy demands that parts are delivered to the next process only as needed, that the parts are of perfect

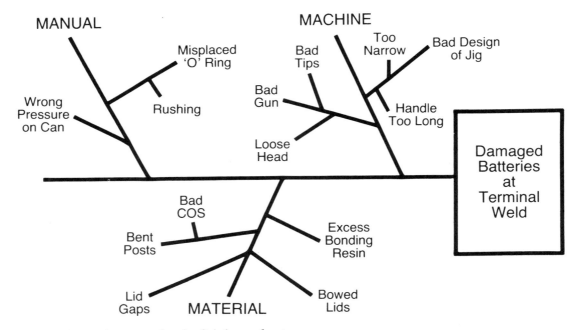

Figure G.1   An example of a fish-bone chart

quality and that there is no waste. The techniques include standardization of designs, focusing the factory and introducing flow into manufacture.

Kanban   Kanban is the Japanese for 'card' or 'signal'. It has become embodied in one of the core JIT techniques of pull scheduling, whereby a manufacturing process signals to a preceding process that it wants more parts. The signal can take the form of cards, tokens, electronic signals, or simply by shouting 'send me some more!' In this way,

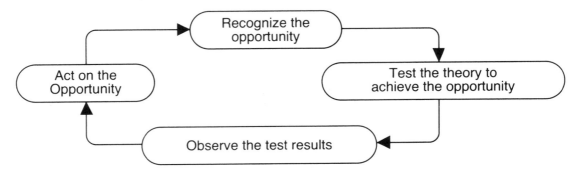

Figure G.2   The Plan-do-check-action, or Shewhart cycle

manufacturing processes can be progressively integrated closely together.

PDCA   The Plan-do-check-action (PDCA) cycle was developed by Walter Shewhart, although it is often called the Deming cycle after W Edwards Deming. It is a 4-step approach to improving what Deming calls 'analytic' problems — those related to the effect of processes on products. The cycle is illustrated in Figure G.2.

Quality Control (QC) Circles   QC Circles are typically six to eight people drawn from a department who volunteer to meet under the leadership of the foreman or department head to identify and solve problems affecting their work. Members are trained in the use of systematic problem-solving techniques such as brainstorming, Pareto analysis and fishbone charts (described above).

Total Quality   Total Quality refers to the involvement of everyone (not just manufacturing) in assuring the quality of the company's products and services. While there is much confusion about definitions between one company and another, the following are two of the more widely accepted definitions.

> **Total quality control (TQC)**   All company members use QC concepts and methods in their work, and thus achieve higher product quality and better results. (Source: Mr H Sahashi, Yuasa Battery UK).

> **Total Quality Management**   This is a process of habitual improvement where control is embedded within, and driven by, the culture of the organization. (Source: M Foster and S Whittle 'The Quality Management Maze', The TQC Magazine, May 1989).

VAN   VAN stands for Value Added Network, and refers to the electronic network used by customers and suppliers to communicate with each other by electronic data interchange (EDI).

Index

BS 7750

Implementing the environment management standard and the EC Eco-management scheme

Brian Rothery

In 1992 the British Standards Institution established BS 7750 as a standard for environmental control in the manufacturing and services sectors. BS 7750 allows organizations to demonstrate that they meet health and safety regulations, local and national environmental requirements and the latest industry codes of practice. Compliance with the Standard will give considerable protection against claims under product liability and against unjustified charges of negligence. Both the impending EC Eco-scheme Regulations and a new ISO Standard are expected to reflect the requirements of BS 7750 and buyers - particularly in public procurement - will begin to look for the Standard in prospective suppliers as they already do for ISO 9000.

Brian Rothery's new book is aimed at senior management, including chief executives, quality managers and all managers responsible for operational processes and for transport and distribution procedures. It explains the background to the Standard and provides a practical guide to installing and maintaining the relevant systems, complete with details of certification procedures. It includes specimen documentation and generic models for the registers and the manual specified by the Standard. The system described is designed to meet the requirements of both BS 7750 and the new EC Eco-management scheme.

1993   256 pages   0 566 07392 7

Gower

Building a Better Team
A handbook for
managers and facilitators

Peter Moxon

Team leadership and team development are central to the modern manager's ability to "achieve results through other people". Successful team building requires knowledge and skill, and the aim of this handbook is to provide both. Using a unique blend of concepts, practical guidance and exercises, the author explains both the why and the how of team development.

Drawing on his extensive experience as manager and consultant, Peter Moxon describes how groups develop, how trust and openness can be encouraged, and the likely problems overcome. As well as detailed advice on the planning and running of teambuilding programmes the book contains a series of activities, each one including all necessary instructions and support material.

Irrespective of the size or type of organization involved, <u>Building a Better Team</u> offers a practical, comprehensive guide to managers, facilitators and team leaders seeking improved performance.

Contents

Introduction • Part I: Teams and Teambuilding • Introduction • Teams and team effectiveness • Teambuilding • Summary • Part II: Designing and Running Teambuilding Programmes • Introduction • Diagnosis • Design and planning • Running the session • Follow-up • Part III: Teambuilding Tools and Techniques • Introduction • Diagnosis exercise • Getting started exercises • Improving team effectiveness exercises • Index.

1993   208 pages   0 566 07424 9

Gower

Empowering People at Work

Nancy Foy

This is a book written, says the author, "for the benefit of practical managers coping with real people in real organizations". Part I shows how the elements of empowerment work together: performance focus, teams, leadership and face-to-face communication. Part II explains how to manage the process of empowerment, even in a climate of "downsizing" and "delayering". It includes chapters on networking, listening, running effective team meetings, giving feedback, training and using employee surveys. Part III contains case studies of IBM and British Telecom and examines the way they have developed employee communication to help achieve corporate objectives.

The final section comprises a review of communication channels that can be used to enhance the empowerment process, an extensive set of survey questions to be selected on a "pick and mix" basis and an annotated guide to further reading.

Empowerment is probably the most important concept in the world of management today, and Nancy Foy's new book will go a long way towards helping managers to "make it happen".

Contents

1994   288 pages   0 566 07436 2

Gower

A Manual for Change

Terry Wilson

Change is now the only constant, as the cliché has it, and organizations who fail to master change are likely to find themselves undone by it.

In this unique manual, Terry Wilson provides the tools for planning and implementing a systematic organizational change programme. The first section enables the user to determine the scope and scale of the programme. Next, a change profile is completed based on twelve key factors. Finally, each of the factors is reviewed in the context of the user's own organization. Questionnaries and exercises are provided throughout and any manager working through these will have not only a clear understanding of the change process but also specific plans ready to put into action.

Derived from the author's experience of working with organizations at every level and in a wide range of industries, the manual will be invaluable to directors, managers, consultants and professional trainers battling to help their organizations survive and flourish in an increasingly turbulent environment.

Contents

1994   230 pages   0 566 07460 5

Gower

Problem Solving
in Groups
Second Edition
Mike Robson

Modern scientific research has demonstrated that groups are likely to solve problems more effectively than individuals. As most of us knew already, two heads (or more) are better than one. In organizations it makes sense to harness the power of the group both to deal with problems already identified and to generate ideas for enhancing effectiveness by reducing costs, increasing productivity and the like.

In this revised and updated edition of his successful book, Mike Robson first introduces the concepts and methods involved. Then, after setting out the advantages of the group approach, he examines in detail each of the eight key problem solving techniques. The final part of the book explains how to present proposed solutions, how to evaluate results and how to ensure that the group process runs smoothly.

With its practical tone, its down-to-earth style and lively visuals, this is a book that will appeal strongly to managers and trainers looking for ways of improving their organization's and their department's performance.

Contents

1993   176 pages   0 566 07414 1 Hardback   0 566 07415 X Paperback

Gower

The Goal

Beating the Competition

Second Edition

Eliyahu M Goldratt and Jeff Cox

Written in a fast-paced thriller style, *The Goal* is the gripping novel which is transforming management thinking throughout the Western world.

Alex Rogo is a harried plant manager working ever more desperately to try to improve performance. His factory is rapidly heading for disaster. So is his marriage. He has ninety days to save his plant - or it will be closed by corporate HQ, with hundreds of job losses. It takes a chance meeting with a colleague from student days - Jonah - to help him break out of conventional ways of thinking to see what needs to be done.

The story of Alex's fight to save his plant is more than compulsive reading. It contains a serious message for all managers in industry and explains the ideas which underlie the Theory of Constraints (TOC) developed by Eli Goldratt - the author described by Fortune as 'a guru to industry' and by Businessweek as a 'genius'.

As a result of the phenomenal and continuing success of *The Goal*, there has been growing demand for a follow-up. Eliyahu Goldratt has now written ten further chapters which continues the story of Alex Rogo as he makes the transition from Plant Manager to Divisional Manager. Having achieved the turnround of his plant, Alex now attempts to apply all that Jonah has taught him, not to crisis management, but to ongoing improvement.

These new chapters reinforce the thinking process utilised in the first edition of *The Goal* and apply them to a wider management context with the aim of stimulating readers into using the technique in their own environment.

| 1993 | 352 pages | 0 566 07417 6 Hardback | 0 566 07418 4 Paperback |

Gower

ISO 9000

Second Edition

Brian Rothery

This is a completely new and revised edition of the highly successful first edition of ISO 9000. This new edition takes account of all of the latest post-1993 changes and additions to the ISO 9000 series of standards, and looks ahead to emerging committee drafts and documents up to 1996.

Some highlights of this new edition are a completely revised generic Quality Manual for manufacturers, which can be taken and customised by any company in manufacturing and design; a brand new services Quality Manual, courtesy ICL, which should be a huge help to service industries adopting the standard; an update on the regulatory situation; and an exposition on how ISO 9000 fits in with other standards and regulations.

This book has been reflecting the worldwide spread of ISO 9000 itself, both in its sales, and in translations. Since first publication it has now become certain that ISO 9000 is the passport for trading, not just within the EC, but throughout the developed world.

The author has pitched the text so that it can be applied to quality managers and decision makers everywhere who are faced with the task of implementing or updating ISO 9000. This new edition will also be very useful for managers who intend also to implement BS 7750, the new environmental management standard, and who need a system to control the compulsory health and safety regulations, as these are cross-referenced to both of these issues.

Finally, the book provides new and penetrating insights into the questions of product liability and the increasingly mandatory nature of management standards such as ISO 9000.

1993   258 pages   0 566 07402 8

Gower